"Having generated over $30m i
selling information courses usin
first-hand how important unde
something Arfa does extraordinarily well in *Mind-Hack™
Marketing.*

Unlike other books that focus primarily on funnel hacks
and mechanics, *Mind-Hack™ Marketing* starts at the very
beginning – diving deep into the psychology of your ideal
customer. The insights inside this book get you thinking more
strategically and will empower you with everything you
need to create high-converting and profitable campaigns
immediately.

Arfa's marketing prowess has impressed me so much that
she's been coaching my high-level mastermind clients who've
been massively benefiting from her incredible wisdom – not
only do they LOVE her, but they're also getting amazing results
from her methods." – **Shaqir Hussyin**, *CEO, FUNNELS.com*

"When it comes to creating high-converting funnel
campaigns, Arfa is my go-to copy ninja! She gets outstanding
results for our clients and is a real pleasure to work with.

Mind-Hack™ Marketing is the most comprehensive deep
dive into the psychology of your customers I've ever come
across. It's packed with actionable takeaways and insights
that will help you create more profitable campaigns.

If you do ANY kind of marketing, then *Mind-Hack™ Marketing* is going to help you skyrocket your success." – **Lisa Catto**, *"The Queen of Automation", thebusinesscatalyst.co.uk*

"As a business coach, I've worked with many small businesses who've struggled because they didn't know how to attract and acquire customers profitably.

That's why I love *Mind-Hack™ Marketing*! It's a MUST for business owners because it gives you a complete blueprint of how to absolutely crush your sales and make your business hyper-profitable.

Arfa's knowledge of marketing is quite simply incredible and she's led several of my mastermind events where her insights for our clients have been nothing short of amazing.

If you're looking for the 'edge' in your marketing and want to take your business to a completely different level, then you need *Mind-Hack™ Marketing*." – **Robin Waite**, *Bestselling Author of "Take Your Shot", Fearless.biz*

"When it comes to the science behind attracting your dream client and understanding the psychology of your audience, Arfa is a genius! Our business model relies heavily on the high-ticket model, and for us, knowing the customer intimately is critical to the success of our business. The strategies inside this book are incredible and have given me and my team a whole new perspective on marketing.

Mind-Hack™ Marketing is in a word BRILLIANT. Whether you're looking for cutting-edge content and ideas or looking for more clarity with your messaging, one thing is certain – this book WILL make you a LOT of money. Five stars and highly recommended!" – *Aaqib Ahmed, CEO, Entrepreneurial Muslim*

"Webinars, Facebook ads, cold calling, networking.

Ever sat down, looking at all the noise in the market, and thought to yourself 'Does any of this stuff actually work, or is it just another marketer trying to sell me some programme that doesn't really work?'

With Arfa, you can be certain this isn't going to be the case.

Arfa is quite humble, so let me do some of the bragging for her and sum it up like this: Arfa eats your favourite marketer for breakfast. With over nine figures generated in her tenure as a freelance copywriter, she's the one that's been creating the campaigns responsible for helping these marketers to explode their own marketing messages.

In short, with *Mind-Hack™ Marketing*, you'll discover the same ninja strategies Arfa has used with her private clients to get them sensational results.

If you have a business, this book is Digital Gold. Grab your pickaxe and be prepared to get insane results!" – *David Stafford, Business Growth Consultant and CEO at David*

"*Mind-Hack™ Marketing* is a marketer's treasure! Arfa is a rare gem in the marketing world and this book is one you won't be able to put down. As marketers, we all know customer psychology plays a big part in marketing…. However, it wasn't until I read *Mind-Hack™ Marketing* that I realised just how many gaps I had in my own business.

I've learned so many new strategies I've never seen anywhere else, and I'm excited to see how my business will progress in the coming months. I'm truly blown away with the clarity and honesty that's laid out inside *Mind-Hack™ Marketing*.

If you want to generate consistent sales in your business, then you need to read this book because Arfa doesn't hold anything back." – **Manny Hanif**, *Social Media Specialist, Hashtagacademy.com*

ISBN: 9798489767293

Imprint: Independently published

This book was produced in collaboration with Write Business Results Limited. For more information on their business book, blog and podcast services, please visit www.writebusinessresults.com or contact the team via info@writebusinessresults.com.

Mind-Hack™ Marketing

How to Turn Customer Psychology into Breakthrough Sales

By Arfa Saira Iqbal

Acknowledgements

With deepest gratitude and praise first and foremost to my Creator who has blessed me with everything I have.

Thank you to my incredible family who've supported me every step of the way. I'm forever grateful for you all and love you all so much.

Asima – my sister, my best friend and my absolute rock. Thank you for putting up with me and having the patience of a saint with helping me get this book out there.

Kevin Hall – my incredible coach who has always pushed, guided, challenged me and helped me get out of my own way. Thank you for believing in me – I'm not even sure this book would have been possible without your unwavering support.

David Stafford – my amazing mentor who has helped me push myself when I didn't want to. You're awesome and I could never repay what you've done for me.

Michael Lassen – my wonderful mentor and marketing coach. Thank you for giving me the courage and the nudge to complete this book!

Dan Bradbury – my trusted adviser. Thank you for supporting me when I needed it most. I'm truly blessed to have met you.

Paul Hancox – my outstanding copy coach. You allowed me

to stand on my own two feet when I was stuck between a rock and a hard place. Just know I'll forever be grateful for your help.

And last but by no means least, to my wonderful clients whom I'm proud to call friends. You've been instrumental in helping cheer me on in getting this book out there!

Dedication

This book is dedicated to my beautiful boys Jamal and Amaan without whom life has no meaning. You've made me who I am and continually drive me to push myself. I love you both from the depths of my soul.

Contents

Foreword by Dan Bradbury

New customers are the lifeblood of your business. If you're looking at growing your business, you're probably all too familiar with the challenges that go with it – from trying to find new markets to competing in existing ones.

Regardless of how great your product or service is, the reality is that it's getting harder and harder to stand out in an increasingly competitive marketplace. And herein lies the greatest challenge – making yourself relevant to your audience.

With over a decade of experience working with hundreds of businesses ranging from low six figures to multi-eight figures, I can tell you that more businesses go broke when trying to grow than for any other reason.

Why? Because most business owners don't know how to acquire customers profitably. There are two key elements at play here: knowing your numbers and understanding your customers. Truth be told, knowing your numbers will only take you so far – because what most business owners forget is that behind every number and behind every metric is a person.

That's where the real breakthrough and the real magic happens. Knowing your customer better than they know themselves and understanding how to translate this knowledge into hyper-profitable campaigns is the "secret sauce" behind uber-successful businesses – and this is exactly what Arfa excels in.

I first met Arfa in 2014 through our flagship Success Mastermind programme. Back then, she was a project manager for a niche matchmaking service that was looking to grow profitably. From the outset, I was immediately impressed by Arfa's deep knowledge and expertise in direct response marketing and her ability to create high-converting campaigns based on the psychology of her target audience.

Arfa's in-depth insights of the ideal customer really blew me away – so much so, that when she decided to move on and go it alone, I immediately asked her to come and work with my team. Over the years, I've seen Arfa really take the concept of the ideal customer to another level.

From delivering sessions to our high-level mastermind clients, to running her amazing avatar workshop, Arfa's unique approach to marketing has made a real difference to the businesses that implement her teachings. I've seen first-hand how she's produced spectacular results for her clients. Whether you've been marketing for a few weeks or for a few decades, you'll find gems inside this book that will help you elevate your marketing campaigns and ultimately make you more money.

Mind-Hack™ Marketing isn't another shiny object. It's NOT a tactical approach to marketing either. It's an entire methodology that starts with the end in mind: your ideal customer. I fundamentally believe that the strategies you'll find inside this book will change the way you look at your marketing forever.

If you're serious about radically levelling up your marketing prowess so you can grow and scale your business confidently, look no further than *Mind-Hack™ Marketing*.

Dan Bradbury
Business Growth Consultant
DanBradbury.com

Preface

For many businesses, marketing seems like an ever-expansive black hole, where money seems to disappear quite quickly – and that's because it's becoming increasingly difficult to stand out online.

Since 2020 when the coronavirus pandemic hit, millions of businesses took the opportunity to move their business online, and the word "pivot" became one of the most overused phrases that year.

Being unable to trade in the usual way simply encouraged savvy business owners to shift the way they did business. While being online is a big opportunity, the opportunity doesn't come without risks.

For example, now, more than ever, you have to contend with an increase in:

- Ads and rising ad costs.
- Emails being sent (my inbox is flooded with hundreds of emails a day!).
- Spam (despite GDPR and SPAM laws, my inbox still gets a ton of junk!).
- Competition.
- Noise in the online space!

All this means your message may well be getting LOST in the process...

And when this happens, you'll never make the kind of money you could be making.

In fact, you'll burn more of your hard-earned money on wasted ad spend that fails to convert. You'll struggle with lower engagement and lower conversions in your sales campaigns.

Most businesses that fail to get their sales campaigns to convert, feel the answer lies in some magic trick – some new marketing trick, tool or hack that other successful business owners are using...

It's one of the biggest reasons why businesses struggle with **shiny object syndrome** – a phenomenon that results in wasting money on the wrong thing because it happens to be the latest or the greatest thing since sliced bread...

When in actual fact, the underlying reason for their failure to convert clicks into paying customers is a lack of understanding about who their customer is.

Long term, these issues will compound and become detrimental to the growth of your business.

And that's where this book comes in. I wrote this book to help you navigate through the noise online and produce campaigns that convert – and do so consistently.

If you serve a select segment of the market, I'm going to show you how you can double down on this, set yourself up for success, and win with your audience.

What's interesting is that the success of businesses that are succeeding is very often placed in the hands of people like myself.

As a direct response copywriter and marketing consultant, it's my job to find new and exciting ways to market the offers my clients create. I'm responsible for finding new angles, positioning products in really exciting ways and making everything sound incredible so that potential customers feel compelled to buy.

While business owners are spoilt for choice in HOW they can market, powerful and effective marketing can only happen when a business understands the audience they are serving – and more importantly, dives deep into the challenges, pain points, desires, fears and frustrations of their target market.

You can have an enormous list of customers with extremely low engagement, which translates into very little money; and you can equally have a tiny list that is hyper-responsive and buys everything you sell them – and all because you took the time to understand your ideal customers.

My job is simple. I'm going to show you EXACTLY what you need to do to transform customer psychology into breakthrough sales. I call this process "Mind-Hacking" because you've got to first get into the mind of your ideal customer and understand what makes them tick BEFORE you can create winning campaigns. This is the premise behind the concept of Mind-Hack™ Marketing.

Mind-Hack™ Marketing is about making the needs of your ideal customer TOP PRIORITY and the driving force behind ALL of your marketing campaigns. In fact, ALL of your content, social media posts, lead magnets, tripwires, ad campaigns, sales funnels and everything in between should be *100% guided by the needs of your ideal customer*.

Key business decisions, such as offering new products and services and creating new marketing campaigns, should NEVER be discussed in isolation without going back to your ideal customer and figuring out what they need BEFORE you start creating new offers.

The businesses that understand their ideal customer (also known as their customer avatar) in detail are the businesses that will make the most amount of money AND create lifelong loyalty with their audience.

In fact, understanding your ideal customer is the difference between businesses that make six figures and businesses that make seven or more figures a year.

If you already have an ideal customer or avatar in place in your business, you're already ahead of the game; if you don't, you NEED to prioritise this over everything else you do...

Because once you know who your avatar is, you can then start changing your:

- Messaging
- Processes
- Systems
- Offers
- Content

And just about any touchpoint you have with your customers! Your avatar is going to guide practically EVERYTHING you do going forward – even how you interact with your customers.

Now I get it: if you've spent months or even years perfecting your systems and your marketing, I promise you do NOT need to change EVERYTHING.

Just a few small tweaks and changes in your existing campaigns may be ALL you need to make a difference – and the benefits will last you a lifetime.

That's why in this book, I'll be sharing with you the EXACT same strategies and principles I've developed and successfully used with my private clients since 2010.

If you've previously struggled or are struggling to sell your offers effectively, or you're looking to scale, then this book is about to become your best friend. I've included plenty of action points throughout to help you see real results with your campaigns.

At the end of this book, I've also included a list of resources to help you on your journey.

Let's dive in!

Arfa Saira Iqbal

Introduction: The Cause of My Epic Business Failure (Embarrassing Admission)

I have an embarrassing admission to make.

Several years back, I made a really bad business decision which meant I spent the next few years deep in debt – and it nearly killed me paying it off.

I did a few online training courses on selecting a particular niche and decided that because I had an interest in alternative health, it would be a good fit for me to focus on the health and wellness industry. In particular, I wanted to help health coaches build a more profitable business.

I spent thousands of pounds (which I borrowed from my family) to start this new venture. Excitedly, I joined a group coaching programme to build the assets I needed for my business: a website, an online presence and a list.

I spent weeks getting every single thing right and felt proud to show my coach what I'd achieved. I then needed help in refining my messages and getting the marketing perfect and on-point – so I hired a strategist who taught me some amazing strategies to help me with that too...

When an opportunity came up to attend a trade show aimed at health and wellness experts, I jumped at the chance, thinking I'd be getting in front of my ideal audience.

The whole idea behind the show was for me to book appointments for free consultations where I would review people's websites for them for free and give them the next steps in creating a powerful client-attracting business.

I was so excited at the prospect of helping my ideal clients get THEIR ideal clients... but it didn't turn out the way I expected.

The trade show itself was quite an event and had around 10,000 people coming through the doors. My assistant (my sister!) and I spent two exhausting days on our feet, talking to potential clients and giving tons of value. We were shattered and our feet were so badly swollen at the end of the day we could barely walk...

However, that didn't matter because I had booked a total of 46 appointments! All I needed to do was convert TWO leads into paying customers and I would be in profit... easy right?

After two difficult days, a lot of travel and a serious amount of expense, I arrived back home on fire and eager to help people on the calls.

Over the next two weeks, I meticulously called each and every single person, spending 30 minutes a pop with them, giving value and helping them find the hidden profits in their business.

My value proposition was based on helping them to build

a super-profitable business and have an amazing online presence, and getting them totally booked up and charging what they were worth. Who wouldn't want that right?

I was confident I had given enough value and help that people would want to do business with me.

But they didn't.

So what went wrong?

The packages I was selling started at around £2,000, which is a serious investment for a startup and even more serious for someone who really doesn't have the money to pay you.

The excuses started rolling in: *I have no money, I need to speak to my business partner, I'll be ready to start when X happens, my friend has just passed away...* you get the idea!

The end result? Not. One. Single. Sale.

I was devastated.

Here I was, a struggling single mother with two kids to raise and what I thought was my last-ditch attempt at making this business work (using money that didn't even belong to me), and it totally failed.

Despite obliterating every objection, offering payment plans and doing follow-up calls, all I ended up with was wasted time, effort and money on a segment of the market that didn't have the funds to grow their business.

Key lesson – my business failed on an epic scale because I didn't stop to consider the psychology of my customer.

Here's the thing: people in the health and wellness industry are great at helping others, but not so great at helping themselves. That's why so many health coaches struggle to make money – because they don't invest what's needed to make their business work.

My services were WAY out of the price range of every single person I spoke to. And even if they had the money, it was way too scary for them to think about; and deep down, they didn't believe they could have the results they so desperately wanted.

When you invest in yourself at a higher level, it goes without saying that you have to step up your game. You can't hide or play small. The very nature of investing at a higher level requires you to do things that are not easy and are hard work; and not everyone is at this level.

And this was something I didn't understand about my prospects. Had I taken the time to really understand the psychology of my prospects, I would have understood that a smaller, entry-price service that's easy to consume and implement would have given my audience the confidence and the ability to get results. And then, when they were ready, they could upgrade to a higher package and see even better results.

This is where the whole concept of understanding your customer took off for me. The strange thing was that when I wrote copy for clients, I relied heavily on psychology to make the sale. However, with this venture, I was so wrapped up in getting everything right that I missed the biggest trick of all: knowing what made my market tick and understanding their fears as well as their hopes and desires.

The experience I had with this particular business idea was so devastating that I had no choice but to take on a proper job (on a monthly retainer) just so I could feed my kids and pay my rent. Despite the serious blow it gave to my confidence, this experience propelled me (unbeknown to me at the time) to develop the system I have today.

In business, there's actually no such thing as failure. Only lessons learned. And boy did I learn a heavy lesson!

Understanding how your prospects and customers think is critical to the success or failure of your business.

In fact, I would go as far as to say that ANY business that serves a particular segment of the market but fails to understand it, will NEVER be able to achieve the kind of growth and impact it wants to achieve, without this core skill.

Knowing your customer at a deep level empowers you to make the right decision for every aspect of your business – including the marketing methods you choose.

Here's how understanding your customers can truly help

your business grow:

- Drives down the cost of your ads and your marketing.
- Eliminates tyre-kickers and people who waste your time.
- Dramatically improves conversion rates in all your marketing campaigns.
- Increases engagement in your emails.
- Helps you to understand which products or services your audience actually wants, needs and will buy.
- Helps you build powerful campaigns using tools like Keap (InfusionSoft), Kartra, Clickfunnels or any other automation software.
- Prevents list burnout and reduces spam complaints.
- Increases trust and authority in the mind of your prospects about your business.
- Increases the number of sales you make.
- Allows you to get in front of the people who will be happy to pay for your stuff, at the price you command.
- Increases your profits and decreases unnecessary and wasteful marketing spend.
- Opens up new revenue streams for you.
- Ultimately makes you more money!

In short, understanding your customers underpins your entire business model and forms the foundation on which your business can successfully grow.

Had I really taken the time to understand the psychology of the market I went after, I wouldn't have ended up in such a huge mess that took me almost four years to clean up.
Yes, you read that right: **four whole years!**

It is by far the most difficult and painful lesson I've ever had to learn in business, bar none. But this is exactly what this book is about. My experience forced me to get super smart about the way I do business.

Everything, from my business model to my niche to the very words I use to promote my business, has changed based on the needs of my ideal client.

In fact today, my experience of understanding the deeper psychology of how people think and behave has enabled me to run an incredibly profitable business in which I've helped make my clients over eight figures (and counting!).

Uncovering the truth about your market and your ideal customer is, without a doubt, one of the fastest and easiest ways to make more money in your business WITHOUT increasing ad spend or wasting money on endless campaigns that fail to convert. This is why *Mind-Hack™ Marketing* is so powerful.

Even if you only apply some of the principles you'll learn in this book, you'll see **a remarkable improvement in your engagement and sales** – and you won't even need to spend additional money on advertising to benefit!

Mind-Hack™ Marketing is designed to help you not only increase your profitability and drive down your marketing spend, but also to help you build a powerful relationship with your audience.

You've probably heard marketers say that the money's in the list... but actually, that's not true.

The money is in the relationship you have with your list.

The more you understand your audience, the better you can serve them and give them what they need.

Once you do this, you'll build the know, like and trust factor, and people will see you as an authority in your industry.

The principles in this book will give you a blueprint for successfully moving a complete stranger into a repeat customer and raving fan – and all because you took the time to understand what they wanted and needed.

You'll learn how getting inside the mind of your potential customers can easily double or even triple your sales without increasing your ad spend.

By understanding what makes your customers tick, you'll be able to create customer-specific ad campaigns, marketing funnels and unique customer journeys based on their needs.

This is your complete marketing roadmap which is going to give you the clarity you need around all of your marketing.

You'll stop wasting time and money on ads and campaigns that target the wrong people and fail to convert.

Here's what you're going to discover:

- **Mind-Hack™ Method** – Get into the mind of your potential customers by understanding the psychology of buying behaviour, such as objections, motivations, desires, fears and beliefs. Create emotionally driven and powerful campaigns that connect with your prospects and dramatically improve sales.

- **Learn how to build out your avatar and persona profiles** – Get down to the deeper reasons behind what motivates your prospects to buy.

- **Continual Sales Loop™** – Learn more than a dozen different ways in which you can sell the same product or service to your audience without creating "list fatigue".

- **Perpetual Profit System™** – From your ads to your sales funnels, and from your content to social media, you'll learn how to use your avatar information to create a powerful system that continuously converts and makes you money even while you sleep!

This book is based on my signature **Mind-Hack™ Marketing** workshop where I personally teach business owners how to understand their customers over two intense days.

This book is going to give you everything you need to successfully create your marketing campaigns, content marketing, sales funnels, and everything else in between!

It's the PERFECT place to start if you want to maximise your success with tools such as Keap (InfusionSoft), Clickfunnels or other automation software. It's also the ideal place to begin if you're looking at creating any kind of marketing campaign and you want it to be profitable.

As a side note, I'll be using "clients" and "customers" interchangeably. I'll also use a lot of weight loss examples throughout this book because it's very easy to understand and explain.

Let's get started!

Part 1: It All Starts With Your Customer

It pays to start with the end in mind. Nowhere is this more relevant than in business – particularly when you're marketing and selling your products and services. The end goal of marketing is to acquire a customer and turn the customer into a repeat buyer.

Everything you do in business is centred around selling profitably by maximising the lifetime value of your customer.

That's why it makes sense to ensure you really know the pain points, struggles, aspirations, motivations and desires of your target market. In today's fast-paced world where you're only one click away from your competitors, it pays to be relevant to your customers.

Think of relevancy like currency – your ideal customers have an unmet need. You have an offer that's perfect for them. When the product-to-market fit is perfect, there's an exchange of energy. Money for the goods.

Mind-Hack™ Marketing is about showing you how to increase your relevancy by really digging deep into the psychology of your target market. And that's what this part of the book is all about.

Over the next few chapters, I'll show you how to figure out the needs of your audience and how to go DEEP into their emotions to figure out what makes your customers tick. When you finally understand why your audience is REALLY buying from you, your perspective on marketing will really shift.

Chapter 1: The Psychology of Buying Behaviour

In this chapter, we'll discuss the psychology of buying behaviour, also known as psychographics. Put simply, this is the message you give to your audience through all of your marketing efforts — be it through email newsletters, social media posts, lead magnets, trip wires, and everything in between.

Specifically, we're going to be covering the deeper reasons why people buy — like identity, feeling and function. We're also going to be looking at the reasons why people don't buy, their objections and what's actually preventing them from literally opening up their wallets and giving you their money. I call this process the Mind-Hack™ Method because I systematically show you how to dig deep into the needs of your ideal client.

The other day, I was scrolling through my newsfeed on Facebook and an ad popped up telling me how to market "my" baby business properly. This really annoyed me for a few reasons...

First, I don't have a baby business. The language used in the ad implied that I did. Second, it was clear this person didn't have a clue about how to market her own business... so then how could she possibly help anyone else with theirs?

And third, I must have seen this ad appear in my newsfeed

not once, but several times. This really annoyed me because it felt like the equivalent of walking into a shop and being asked several times if I would like to buy something I didn't want.

Think about this for a moment. If this happened in real life, you'd probably run out of the store as fast as possible (and would likely never return!).

And yet this is PRECISELY what many businesses do when advertising online and they don't even know it. In fact, it's NOT just when advertising. It's in how you talk to your customers, how you interact with them and how you share or convey information with them.

The primary reason this happens at all is because most business owners don't understand who their target market is.

You've probably heard the term "ideal customer" many times before; however, did you know there is a direct, positive correlation between businesses that know and understand their ideal customer really well and the amount of money they make?

So what exactly does that mean and how does understanding your ideal customer REALLY impact your business?

If your business serves a particular segment of the market, then you REALLY need to pay attention to this, because it's essential to your success.

Everything you'll learn in this book can be applied to almost any industry, including the corporate market. I'll show you how you can leverage this understanding to make more money in your business WITHOUT spending more on advertising.

For most business owners, their primary focus is naturally on selling more of their products and services. This usually means increasing the number of customers, selling them more goods and getting them to come back more often.

It's important to understand that you can ONLY ever increase your sales in one of three ways:

1) Increase Customers

Of all the activities a business will engage in, acquiring customers has the greatest cost attached to it. The process of getting a paying customer starts with finding the right prospects, getting them to become a lead, and then eventually converting leads into paying customers.

In essence, this is what a sales funnel is (we'll discuss this later in Chapter 9!). Your job as a business owner is to create awareness of your products and services and then turn that awareness into leads and sales.

It can be a long and sometimes complicated process and involves a mix of content, paid, referral, social media and email marketing. As I said before, the most amount of money is spent in acquiring a customer.

However, this creates a problem – one that you might be familiar with....

Unfortunately, there's the assumption that doubling the traffic to your website will automatically double your sales – and that's not true!

This is flawed thinking and can mean thousands of pounds in wasted ad spend.

Because increasing customers is where the most amount of effort, energy and money is spent, it's therefore absolutely CRITICAL you market to the right people ALL the time. We'll get to this in a moment.

2) Increasing the Average Order Frequency (AOF)

The average order frequency (AOF) simply means the number of times your customers bought from you in any given period.

Getting customers to repeatedly buy from you requires a mixture of having the right offerings that are of value to your ideal customer and then staying in front of them through various means of marketing.

3) Increasing the Average Order Value (AOV)

The average order value (AOV) is simply the average total of every order a customer places with you over a defined period of time. AOV is an important metric for online businesses because it drives key decisions such as advertising spend and product pricing.

Here's the thing – in order for any business to scale and grow to its fullest potential, you need to increase the number of ideal customers you have, the AOV and the AOF.

But, there's a fundamental truth in truly being able to make the kind of money you've always dreamed of, which very few people actually talk about, and that's this:

ALL three of these factors are fully DEPENDENT on how well you understand your customers. PERIOD.

It's All About the Touchy-Feely!

You've heard of the saying "Customer is king", and most people would associate that with how you treat and deal with your customers. But I'd like to throw something that's equally as important into this mix, and that's the importance of feelings.

It's all about how your customer feels. And no, this isn't some wishy-washy statement!

A customer who feels you understand them, who feels valued and, more importantly, feels as if you truly want to help them, will always prefer to do business with you rather than your competitors.

Remember that in the online world, you're literally one click away from your competitors. This is why understanding the needs of your ideal customer is mission critical to the success of your business and why you need *Mind-Hack™ Marketing*.

Many businesses mistakenly think that the trick to scaling and growing is by pumping out more products and reaching more people, when in actual fact, if they just paid attention to WHO they are serving and placed the needs of their ideal customers first, they would grow at an accelerated rate.

Part of the problem is that it's easy to become clinically detached and think of your customers as a number on a spreadsheet, another number on just a list...

So, when you hear marketers harp on about how the money is in the list, it's easy to assume this relates to the size of your list. However, this is far from the truth! In reality, ***the money is in the RELATIONSHIP you build with your list!***

Key business decisions, such as offering new products and services and creating new marketing campaigns, should NEVER be discussed in isolation without going back to your ideal customer and figuring out what they need BEFORE you start creating new offerings! The businesses that get this make the most money!

What Happens if I Don't Understand My Ideal Customer?

Simple – you'll never make the kind of money you could be making. You'll fail to inspire your customers to become lifelong raving fans of what you do. You'll burn more of your hard-earned money on wasted ad spend that fails to convert.

You'll struggle with lower engagement and lower conversions in your sales campaigns.

Long term, these will compound and become detrimental to the growth of your business.

Time to Take Action

Now you know WHY it's important to understand your ideal customer, the next step is to figure out WHO that ideal customer is. For some businesses, this process is easier than others. The more data you have, the easier it is to nail your ideal customer or avatar.

In the next section, we'll do a deep dive on figuring out your ideal customer. For most businesses, they have a good idea of who that looks like – but for some, they don't have a clue.

So for now, the big question is how do you figure out who you serve when you have no idea?

Complete the exercise on the next page to help you figure this out.

Three Ways to Figure Out Your Ideal Customer

Here are three ways to work out who your ideal customer is:

- **Take stock of your customer base** – Spend some time going through your customer lists. Are they predominantly male or female? Do they fall into a particular age bracket? Do you service a particular area? Are your customers educated? If so, how educated? Do they have families? Are they earning over a certain amount? Do they have kids? Write these answers down. You're basically looking for patterns in the demographic information which makes it easier for you to identify your ideal customer.

- **Survey your list** – Figure out who your customers are by asking the right questions. A simple survey to your list (offer an incentive in order to increase responses) is a great way to find out more about your target market. Use a tool like SurveyMonkey or even Google Forms to create and send surveys. If your business requires customers to create an account, you can just add a simple form as part of the sign-up process to get this information.

- **Keep an eye on competitors** – If you're having a hard time figuring out who you serve, look at your more successful competitors. What kind of ads are they running? What kind of people are they attracting? A good way to do this is to look at their social media accounts – especially Facebook. Figure out who the majority of their fans are and you'll get an idea of who your target market should also be.

TOP TIP – Focus only on the MAJORITY or around 80% of your customers, rather than getting caught up in the unique differences of every single customer. You're looking for themes or patterns that are very obvious.

For example, if you're a dog trainer, you know immediately that your target market is dog owners. They might be primarily female, in the 20–40 age bracket and have families. They may be living in your local area and have a large disposable income.

Once you've done this exercise, you should have a better and clearer picture of who your ideal customer is. You can use this information when running ads on platforms such as Facebook to ensure that you're targeting your ads to the right group of people.

This one change alone will automatically make your ads more relevant, more targeted and will get you better results with your campaigns because the right people are seeing your offer.

We'll go deep into avatars later on, but for now, this exercise should have at least stimulated some thinking on your WHO.

The Pain and Pleasure Principle

Understanding who you're going to market to is scratching the surface of what you need to know in order to create effective marketing campaigns. An important principle we need to consider is the *Pain and Pleasure Principle* which will underpin the majority of your marketing.

Developed by famous neurologist Sigmund Freud, the *Pain and Pleasure Principle* simply means that people work harder to move away from pain than they do towards pleasure, which is why most marketers choose to focus on moving people away from pain.

For example, let's say you have someone who hates their job, and your product is going to show them how they can be really wealthy, buy the house of their dreams and never worry about money again. While they may well love the idea, they might also think it sounds too good to be true and that it's not attainable.

Selling your product in this instance might prove to be difficult; however, if you use the principles of pain and pleasure, you can create compelling reasons why the prospect might buy from you.

For instance, you might say that by purchasing your product or service, your prospect is no longer going to be a slave to the nine to five, they'll be able to spend more time with their family and they'll be able to do the things they've been putting off for years. By focusing on the pain and the pleasure, you're more likely to motivate prospects to purchase from you.

Keep a balance in how you talk about your product. Pain is a powerful motivator, but you don't want to scare your prospects either. Fear is a powerful driver – however, it has a tendency to make people do one of the following:

- *Fight* – Face the problem head on (which only a small percentage of wpeople will do).
- *Flight* – Run away from the problem.
- *Freeze* – Do nothing.

So while it's important to talk about the pain points, you

need to balance this by showing people what life is like on the other side of that pain.

Great marketing campaigns paint a very clear picture of what pain and pleasure look like, but they don't go overboard with the pleasure or too intense with fear. As I've said, the latter will put your prospects off from wanting to do business with you.

Action Points
Answer these questions in relation to your product or service:

1. What does your prospect want the most?
2. What does your prospect fear or hate the most?
3. Where is your prospect currently and where would they like to be?

The answers to these questions will give you a good place to start with your campaigns.

Relationships – The Missing Connection

It's official: every day millions of businesses are sabotaging their own results and cheating themselves out of additional profits by violating a simple rule of marketing – connection.

Let me explain: in 2020, auditing company BDO LLP[1] cited the top 10 reasons why businesses fail, with "not understanding your customers' value" being the number one reason.

Basically, the businesses that will survive are those businesses that have a strong customer proposition – regardless of which kind of business you're in. What does this mean in practical terms?

Simply put, it means that unless you're in the business of educating, helping and being committed to connecting and engaging with your prospects, you'll fail to survive.

Information has become a social currency with which you can buy and earn trust from your ideal customers.

Now I want you to take a long, hard look at your own business model and answer these questions:

- What are you doing to establish a connection with your clients and your prospects?
- How are you treating your prospects when they come into your world?
- How are you using your expertise to HELP them make an informed decision?

The truth is that unless you establish a deep connection with your prospects by helping them understand what you do and

---

[1] BDO United Kingdom, "The top 10 reasons for business failure", *BDO*, 9 March 2020, available at: https://www.bdo.co.uk/en-gb/insights/locations/manchester/the-top-10-reasons-for-business-failure

understand how you can help them, the likelihood of them going to your competitors who DO offer deeper value is very high. It's known as "relationship marketing" or "value-based marketing" and is something that people in the good old days were very good at.

When I was a kid, my mother would go to the fishmonger on the high street if she wanted fish. The fishmonger would advise her on which type of fish was best for which dish. He would make suggestions on how to cook the fish for the best results.

In other words, the fishmonger would do a form of consulting and it was a very personalised service.

Fast forward to the modern-day world where convenience and speed are key. Don't get me wrong, people still value speed and convenience, but now the problem is that the human touch is missing. You can walk into any large supermarket and buy fish readily in the frozen food aisle.

Of course you have the option of going to the fish counter if they have one, but you also have the choice of speaking to the fishmonger... and you'll pay extra for their service.

People who value the expertise of the fishmonger will happily pay for the benefit of having freshly caught fish prepared in store so they can ask for advice on how to cook it well. What's important here is that customers should be given a choice.

You might be wondering, "So what's this got to do with my business?"

Let me tell you. If you're not actively trying to build a relationship with your prospects and you're only interested in selling to them, it's going to eventually backfire. People no longer respond to constant email messages telling them to buy this to get rich or get well or anything else of that nature.

Do that and your potential prospects will hit the unsubscribe button faster than you ever thought possible. Your first and foremost move should always be to come from a place of help and service to your potential prospect.

Be open and honest from the outset – you're there to help your prospects have a better understanding of HOW they can be helped. Always remember, it's not about YOU – it's about them. I'm not saying that you should not pitch to them at all, but what I AM saying is that you should establish the value of what you do FIRST, before asking for their trust in the form of a sale.

In essence, this is all this really is: an exchange of energy (in the form of money) for the trust in your business. And you have to pre-sell your services and deliver on that trust. What tips and advice can you give them, or what free training calls and reports can you send them that will position YOU as the authority in your industry and enable them to make a choice based on "natural selection"?

If you always remember these factors when doing your

marketing, you'll create a community of fans who choose to stay with you based on the value you offer, rather than collecting digital dust in their spam folder. Later in the book, I'll share some inside secrets on increasing the number of emails that get opened and read.

So Why Don't People Buy?

It might sound obvious but unless you have a really clear understanding as to why people aren't buying from you, you won't be able to fix the problem. So the first thing that you need to be aware of is that it's **rarely** about the money!

Unless you're selling something like a house or a car or something that's a considered purchase, money is rarely a reason to say no. In actual fact, it's more to do with how people feel internally and the thought processes that are surrounding that particular area of their life that they're struggling with.

It could also be because there are certain things you're doing (or not doing) in your marketing that's not helping them make a decision. One of the key drivers in getting people to take any form of action is that you've done a good job in articulating how well your product or service can help them. Failure to do that means your prospects have incomplete or missing information – and this can stop them from buying from you.

Missing Call to Action (CTA)

One of the most common things I see is not having a CTA. A CTA is a call to take an action, and is designed to move prospects into making a decision.

If you don't ask clearly for the sale, you're not going to get it. This may sound a little simplistic, but test after test has proven that if you don't ask people to take an action, they won't do it or they'll put off the decision to do it. The truth is prospects are always looking for the easy option in everything – and this includes making buying decisions.

For example, if you want them to download something, you have to be really clear about the actions they need to take. So, let's say you've got a video on your webpage with a sign-up form to the right of it and you want people to fill it out. You literally need to tell them: *"There's a sign-up form to the right of this video. Just enter your name and email address, and then click the 'download now' button."* That's how clear you need to be.

A call to action doesn't just have to be related to purchasing something. It may be that you want someone to schedule a call, download a free e-book or give some feedback. Whatever it is, you've got to clearly articulate it. And if you don't have a clear call to action, you're risking lower conversion rates.

There are two kinds of CTAs: Transitional and Direct.

Transitional CTA – Also known as a soft call to action, this requires your audience to learn more about what you do. The focus is on giving value and creating a relationship before you do business with them, and examples include:

- Downloading a lead magnet
- Taking a free trial
- Signing up for a webinar
- Arranging a free consultation.

Direct CTA – This is where you're asking your audience to do business with you. An effective CTA tells people exactly what to do, such as:

- Buy Now
- Add to Cart
- Donate Now.

Action Points
- Ensure your homepage has both direct and transitional CTAs on it.
- Add an appropriate CTA in ALL of your free content.
- Keep your CTA visible in the navigation menu on your website at all times.
- Be clear – tell people exactly what to do in order to take you up on your offers e.g. "Click the red button below this video to download your free guide."

No Want or Need

Another reason why people don't buy is that they simply don't want or need your product. It's not that they don't want or need the solution (they do), but they may not need or want what YOU have to sell. It may well be that you need to tweak your product or service to better fit their needs. Think about what the big problems are that your product solves and ask yourself if you're doing a good enough job of articulating the value of what you offer.

How will it change your prospect's life? What pain will it help them avoid? How will their life change as a result of your solution? Are you spelling ALL of this out clearly enough in your marketing and your content?

Prospects Don't Know HOW to Buy or What Happens Next

People don't buy when you don't show them how to buy. This is a little bit different to a call to action because this is more about showing people in a sequential way how to purchase something, and it's also about setting expectations.

For example, if the order process is confusing and you haven't explained it properly, you're going to lose people out of sheer frustration. Even if they want the item, they're not going to bother.

Amazon do a fantastic job of this despite the fact they have millions of items on their website. So when you look at their site, it will say things like "Buy now with one click" or "Get it tomorrow if you order in 3 hours 56 minutes" etc. They are very, very clear about what is going to happen if you click on any given button, so there's no confusion for the customer.

Similarly, setting expectations is also critical. If someone places an order and it's going to take several weeks to arrive, the LAST thing you want to do is leave customers hanging in the dark and wondering when their item is going to arrive.

For example, my sister ordered a mattress from a company who made it very clear that delivery would take five to six weeks. Now after spending £800 on a mattress, you'd think the company would try harder at keeping in touch with their customers. Long story short – my sister cancelled the order four weeks in because, in her own words, there was "radio silence" from the company and she wasn't impressed.

She expected regular emails and updates about her order and she got nothing. Placing an order online is STILL a matter of trust – especially when people are dealing with a company they've never heard of. During the decision-making process, some companies are exceptional when it comes to wowing prospects… but the second a sale happens, it's like they don't care any more.

It's a bit like dating – when you meet someone you like and you want to impress them, you'll do whatever it takes to make them happy… and then when they've committed to you and married you, it doesn't take a genius to work out what would happen if you suddenly stopped showing interest in them and stopped communicating with them!

The same is true in business. Don't take your customers for granted. What happens AFTER the sale is just as important as what happens BEFORE the sale. If you don't communicate effectively after the purchase, **buyer's remorse** sets in very quickly. Buyer's remorse is when your customers regret making the purchase. It's one of the big reasons why people complain and/or get refunds.

Here are some ways you can prevent buyer's remorse:

- **Add value before they buy from you** – Sharing great content, how-to tutorials, tips and hacks.
- **Affirm customers have made the right decision** – A simple email congratulating customers on making a smart decision to buy from you is a great way to help.
- **Keep talking** – You can even tell customers how to get the most out of the products they've bought and continue to nurture your customers with great content so they're more likely to repeat buy from you.
- **Set expectations** – Nothing's worse than radio silence or not knowing what's coming next. Be CLEAR on what's coming up or going to happen so there aren't any surprises.
- **Make it easy for customers to contact you** – Don't make customers jump through hoops to contact you. They should CLEARLY understand how to get in touch if there is a problem.
- **Appreciate your customers** – Sending thank you notes with their order, offering loyalty discounts, offering member-only surprise bonuses and gifts are all ways to thank customers and keep them coming back for more.
- **Onboard customers where appropriate** – Some business

models would benefit from an onboarding process. For example, if you have a high-level consulting service, get clients into a welcome session and share some amazing information, or even give them a bonus welcome coaching call to help get them started in your process as painlessly as possible.

They Don't Trust You

Another reason why people don't buy is they don't trust you – period. You can see evidence of this in your own purchasing decisions. Let's say you want to buy a laptop and there's some brand you've never heard of alongside an Apple Mac. Even if the unfamiliar laptop has a better spec and price than the Mac, the likelihood is you'd probably go for the Mac because you trust the brand.

With an unknown brand, there is no trust factor because of uncertainty. When you've never heard of a brand before, you have no idea if it's any good. If the product in question has a lack of reviews thrown into the mix, it confirms any suspicions in your mind that perhaps this product isn't any good, even though that might not be true.

People don't buy when they are uncertain because it creates a feeling of unease. Usually when people have a lack of trust in you and your product it's because you haven't done a good enough job of really selling yourself, your vision, what you stand for, etc. You've not talked enough about how you help people overcome their problems. You haven't got enough social proof by way of reviews, case studies and testimonials.

In other words, you don't have enough evidence to create a solid enough case for people to trust you and buy from you. You can have the best product in the world, but unless you can demonstrate WHY it's so good and back it up with proof, the likelihood of someone purchasing is going to be low.

Fear of Failure

Another reason that prevents your prospect from purchasing from you is a fear of failure. Your prospect doesn't fear that your product will fail, rather they fear THEY will fail. This is critical for you to understand because it's related to the internal psychology of your prospect. What's preventing them from going ahead and investing in themselves? And that's really how you need to think about it.

This is not about your prospects investing in your product. This is about prospects investing in themselves; if they feel that they can't somehow make your product work for them, you're not going to get the sale – no matter how awesome your product actually is. Failing is a conversation going on in their own mind, and your job is to instil confidence within your prospects and help them believe and understand that they CAN succeed with your product.

One of the best ways you can do this is to reframe objections head-on with your prospects. For example, if you're selling a weight loss product and your prospects believe they won't succeed because they're too busy to cook healthy meals, you can turn this into a selling point by ensuring your meal plans can be cooked from scratch within 20 minutes.

The aim is to make the journey as frictionless as possible for your prospects – and the more you obliterate your prospects' objections, the easier you'll find it to make sales.

Make a list of the top objections your prospects have about you and your products and then overcome them in your marketing. A clever example of this is the advertising campaign that car company Avis ran back in 1962.

The car rental company had always trailed behind its number one competitor, Hertz. Worried about the continual losses they were making, Avis hired ad agency Doyle Dane Bernbach to solve this problem for them. The agency did something rather clever. They used Avis' position of always being second as a selling point and came up with the famous, **"When you're only No. 2, you try harder. Or else."**

It was a genius way to tell customers about their amazing customer service. The ad campaign was an instant hit, netting Avis in under a year a cool $1.2 million from previous losses of $3.2 million. The impact on the business was huge, since it was the first time it had been profitable in more than a decade.

You Don't Understand Your Prospects

If your prospects feel you don't understand them, it's unlikely they'll do business with you. Specifically, if they feel you don't understand their pain points, fears, frustrations and the things that worry them most, they'll move onto another brand that does. This is because psychologically, if you can't demonstrate you understand your prospects, they will think you can't help them, which means that ultimately they won't do business with you.

Your Competition Is More Attractive to Your Prospects

People also don't buy from you because they go to your competitors instead – just as we saw in the Apple Mac example earlier. It's not just about trust. It might also be that your competitor is doing a much better job of selling their products and services than you are.

Again, this is about getting people to invest in themselves, so if you're just selling based purely on logic and not addressing the psychology and emotions of your prospect, then you're going to lose the sale. Remember, *people buy on emotion and justify with logic later*[2]. And if your competitor is doing a better job of deeply understanding your customer, they will always win the sale.

It takes minutes to research a product online. Reviews tell you instantly why a product is good compared to its competitor. Businesses that have the most awareness of their market focus all of their time and attention on speaking about the things that their prospects care about the most. They've figured out the reasons why people don't buy from them, and work on fixing and addressing them head on.

---

[2] Michael Harris, (2017), 'Neuroscience Confirms We Buy on Emotion & Justify with Logic & yet We Sell to Mr. Rational & Ignore Mr. Intuitive', Customer Think, 2 April, available at: https://customerthink.com/neuroscience-confirms-we-buy-on-emotion-justify-with-logic-yet-we-sell-to-mr-rational-ignore-mr-intuitive/

You're Pitching It All Wrong

Pitching has an art to it. When you get this wrong, it can turn people off and prevent them from buying from you. Pitching is about adding value FIRST, before you ask for the sale. Give incredible information that is helpful, share tips and advice. Help your prospects learn more about why they are stuck.

When you invest in your prospects BEFORE you ask for the sale, the sale becomes much easier. Imagine going into a department store and being continuously pitched on a product without any real value exchange first. You'd feel as if the store is only after the sale and doesn't care about you.

Your job is to not only give value upfront, but it's also to ensure the pitch is about your prospects and their needs. It's NOT about your product and how awesome it is. Pitching is ALWAYS about the end user – period.

If you can't articulate how your product is going to make your prospect's life easier, you'll pay for it with fewer sales.

Summary

In this chapter, we talked about the psychology of buying behaviour and, specifically, we talked about the following:

- When people don't buy, it's very rarely about the money.
- People will do more to get away from pain than they will to just move towards pleasure (usually)!
- It's your job as a business to articulate the transformation

people will get from your products or services.

In the next chapter, we'll continue to explore how our psychology impacts the way we buy. Specifically, we'll cover how belief systems have a huge impact on a person's buying decision.

Chapter 2: Belief Systems

In this chapter, we're going to be taking a really deep dive into belief systems; internal beliefs versus external beliefs. Beliefs play a HUGE part in the buying cycle. What your customers believe about you and themselves plays a major role in getting people from "I'm thinking about it" to "I need this now!"

When it comes to buying behaviour, people are usually influenced by either **internal beliefs or external beliefs**. These beliefs will determine whether someone will buy or NOT buy from you. This is a crucial part of Mind-Hack™ Marketing – because without this knowledge, you'll never really fully understand what's impacting your prospect's buying decision.

Internal beliefs are things that hold you back in your own mind. External beliefs include anything that impacts the way a person thinks or feels about something.

The things I'm going to be talking about in this chapter are really, really powerful. If you use this information properly, it's going to completely change the way you do business. Essentially, this is a deep dive into the techniques that many famous marketers use to drive sales and profitability.

Internal Beliefs

Internal beliefs refer to the dialogue that's going on inside your prospect's mind before they consider the sale. If you think about your own journey when it comes to buying goods, whether you're aware of it or not, you're weighing up the pros and cons of a particular product before you actually decide to buy.

Now, if you've got certain objections coming up in your mind, then the person who is selling you the item should have done a good enough job of overcoming those objections in order to persuade you to buy. If, however, they've not done a good job, you won't be convinced to buy.

In short, objections are preventing your prospect from opening up their wallets and parting with their money. Like I mentioned earlier, the better you get at trying to overcome objections, the easier it will be for you to make sales. We will be talking about external beliefs later, but for now we're going to be focusing on the things that are preventing your prospect from making that commitment because of internal beliefs.

Lack of Knowledge

Lack of knowledge is simply when somebody doesn't know how to do something to achieve a result they're after. So if you have a weight loss product, it may well be that a person wants to lose weight but they don't actually know how to get started. They don't know what to do, in what order to do it or what to eat.

And that's actually pretty easy to overcome because you can

convey the "how" in your marketing message e.g. *"Follow this easy step-by-step system to consistently lose three pounds a week."* Lack of knowledge is fairly simple to rectify, since you can easily give people the knowledge they need to move forward with a buying decision.

Lack of Confidence

Lack of confidence is huge, since it can really kill your sales. If somebody doesn't have confidence within themselves and they truly believe they can't succeed, it's actually extremely difficult to convince them otherwise. Even if you manage to secure a sale, the thought processes associated with a lack of confidence still continue well after the customer has purchased from you.

In short, they still believe they don't have the confidence to succeed, which means they think they made a mistake. This can lead to buyer's remorse and can result in the customer requesting a refund. Your job is to reaffirm why they made a good buying decision, and to continue to add value and educate the customer to show them how to make the best of their purchase. Empowering people through action can really help with a lack of confidence.

Lack of Ambition

Most people lack real ambition. Dreaming and having real ambition are two very different things. Anyone can dream big, but only those with ambition will be willing to put in the hard work, effort and sacrifice required to actually fulfil those dreams.

While most people would like to be wealthier, fitter and slimmer etc., only a very small percentage of the population is actually willing to do what it takes to have that. Most people don't have the conviction that allows them to follow through on their dreams, which is one of the reasons why people stay in unsatisfying jobs, for example.

Only a small percentage of people will completely turn their life around – and most of the time the catalyst for change is because they've experienced something so painful, they'll do anything NOT to go through that experience again. In other words, they're willing to do what others aren't willing to do in order to achieve their dreams.

The takeaway here is to avoid trying to sell to ambition, because most people just don't have it. Less than 5% of the world's population actually have ambition – these are the Steve Jobs, Bill Gates and Elon Musks of the world. It doesn't take a genius to figure out that the majority of people you meet in life are simply not there.

The smarter way to sell your products is by marketing to desire instead, because everyone has dreams and desires; and if somebody has the desire to do something, they will usually have the motivation to see it through. We'll talk about desire in greater detail later on, but for now you just want to remember that selling to desire is a lot easier than selling to ambition.

Scepticism

People are naturally sceptical of things that sound too good to be true or too easy to achieve. Attaining anything in life usually requires some kind of effort – so anything that seems effortless can really throw your audience off.

On the flipside, it's actually quite easy to overcome; you just need to frame your sales messages in the right way so that people believe your claims. Showing rather than telling is extremely powerful in helping your prospects immediately understand how your product is easier.

However, something you need to be aware of is the "curse of knowledge". This simply means your audience has "too much knowledge" and they won't buy from you because they think they know better than you. Regardless of what you put in front of them, they'll never purchase from you.

For example, one of my private clients had a breakthrough natural product that cured a common condition that 99.9% of the medical community believed to be completely incurable. Because it was common knowledge that this condition couldn't be cured, I advised my client to provide three things: more social proof, education and endorsements.

Here's what this looks like:

- **Go heavy with proof** – Testimonials, reviews, case studies and social proof (including videos, interviews, and so on).
- **Focus on educating** – Creating valuable content that

educates people on their problems creates trust and breaks down existing beliefs a person holds about something.

- **Endorsements** – Asking a known authority, expert or influencer to talk about the product will go a LONG way in helping to build credibility and establish trust with your audience.

Fear of Success

Yes, it's a real thing. Sometimes, when people get closer to success, it scares them. Some people will go through a lot of hard work and effort to achieve a particular goal, and just as they get to the point where they can almost taste or feel the success, they suddenly pull back. This is because they don't trust the process or it's too frightening or overwhelming for them. And this usually comes down to their confidence; it's a conversation that goes on in their own mind and if they don't trust it, they're not going to buy.

Lack of Skills

Lack of skills is an easy problem to overcome especially if you've got a product or service that's going to teach them the skills they need in order to achieve the results they want. You just have to articulate this clearly in your marketing campaigns.

Lack of Trust

Lack of trust is when someone doesn't believe what your product and service can do for them. We're living in a time now where we're literally bombarded with marketing messages and it seems that everyone is selling the next best thing. As a result, there is a natural distrust towards businesses and the process of selling.

People buy from those they trust – period. Authority, credibility and expertise are critical for people to trust you. If someone has a strong level of trust towards you because you're a recognisable name and have authority in your industry, it makes the buying decision much easier because it puts them at ease. They feel they've made a good decision because it's based upon your reputation.

Apple is a really good example of this, because even though their products cost more than the competition, they still have the lion's share of the market due to their outstanding reputation and the trust they've built with their brand. Regardless of what Apple makes, people will always want to purchase from them.

The best way for you to build trust and credibility is to start creating and sharing amazing, valuable content that resonates with your audience; you've really got to show them that you care about helping them. If you're not adding value to your customers or prospects, you're not giving them a reason to trust you, it's as simple as that.

Apathy

People always look for the easy option which in some cases might be to do nothing! A great example is losing weight.

There are millions of people around the world who want to lose weight and NEED to lose weight, but don't do it – even if they know what to do. The big question is WHY? Simply put, it requires too much change and too much effort, which is why people get lazy and put it off. Apathy is difficult to overcome because it's hard to motivate people to take action.

However, what you can do is show prospects what's going to happen if they continue the way they are i.e. if they don't take action and things stay as they are. Using the weight loss example, you could really paint the picture of what will happen if they continue to stay unfit and overweight, such as getting lifestyle-related diseases, being unhappy with their appearance, losing confidence etc.

You really want to paint a vivid picture of the result of their inaction. On the other side of the spectrum, you need to illustrate how their life is going to change if they actually go ahead and purchase your product or service. What difference will it make? What are the benefits they will see? This is really to do with their "before and after" state and we will talk about this in further detail later; however, for now you just need to understand that apathy is a really big reason why people don't buy.

Lack of Commitment

Lack of commitment ties in with apathy but has more to do with how they view the process. When people think something is way too hard for them, it may be they're focusing too much on how long something is going to take. For example, losing weight takes a long time. It can be daunting to embark on a new diet and fitness regime, because it means long-term change. This is especially true if someone has a lot of weight to lose – like 50 or 100 pounds.

The kind of conversations that are going around in their mind are usually that it's way too much weight to lose and they worry about how they're going to cope and manage on this long and difficult journey. There are so many different things going on in their mind, so many excuses as to why they can't commit to losing weight.

Essentially, it boils down to not placing enough importance on resolving the problem. And so, if it's low down on their list of priorities and it lacks importance, your prospect isn't going to want to buy from you. Even if they know their health is suffering and they know they need to sort it out, they'll justify their decision with excuses, such as not having the time, energy or money to commit to the process.

We already know it's very rarely about the money and it's usually more to do with the fact that they haven't placed the problem they're suffering from high enough on their list of priorities to want to solve it.

Lack of Time

Lack of time is huge because we live in a world now where people are busier than ever, and the rise of dual-income households has become the norm. You'll see in most cases now that both people within a relationship tend to be working – sometimes even different shifts – and then they're also trying to fit in time for children (if they have them), socialising, household tasks etc., and so finding time to fit things in is a really big reason why people will not buy from you.

The best way to overcome this (depending on what you're selling) is by making it super quick and easy for your prospect to use your product or service. If somebody has to commit an hour a day to achieve a particular result with your product or service, they're much less likely to go ahead and purchase it if there is a viable alternative that gives them the same result in just 10 minutes a day.

Really think about the format and the medium in which your products are being delivered. Some markets are naturally known to be constrained with time (e.g. new parents), so overcoming the objection of not having enough time is extremely important. What can you do to make your prospect's life easier and save them time? If you don't remember anything else, remember that people pay for speed to solution. If you're offering a particular product or service where a faster, premium version is not available, can you potentially create something that WILL go faster or help customers get started faster?

Stages of Belief

Internal beliefs can have a huge impact on your sales. There are lots of different levels of beliefs surrounding how your product fits in with a person's worldview, and these will much determine whether or not your product is right for them. This is something you really need to be mindful of because if you get this part wrong, even if you have a great product or service, you're going to find it very, very hard to convince people that they want to buy from you.

We've already spoken about internal beliefs, but it's ALSO important to be aware of differing levels of this belief:

Over-Inflated Claims

Over-inflated claims cause a healthy dose of scepticism – especially in industries where everyone has heard pretty much everything you can think of. Two great examples are the weight loss and the "make money online" industry.

For example, you might see a claim that says, "Lose 20 pounds in 10 days by drinking this special tea." Most people are just not going to believe you, since it sounds too good to be true and seems way too hyped up.

It's tough to convince people when something really does sound incredible, and it can actually do more harm than good because people WILL call you out on your claims. If you DO have big claims about a product, you'd better be ready to back them up with hard facts, statistics and reviews. As a general rule, be mindful of the language you're using and tone down claims that might come across as being over-inflated.

Transference

Transference is when your prospect accepts that your

product is possible... but it's not for them. In other words, your prospect believes that other people can do it, but they can't. This is really to do with your prospect's personal preferences.

For example, if your product involves getting people into a gym, you're going to find it almost impossible to convince people who prefer to work out at home to want to come and work out in your studio.

For people who don't go to the gym (but aren't averse to the idea), the right kind of messaging and the right kind of marketing may be able to convince them to give it a go.

Confidence to Achieve the Result

While we've already covered a lack of confidence, there is a different level of confidence where someone believes what you're offering is achievable but not by them. They can't do it because there's something inside telling them they're not quite ready to take this on. This is huge – especially in the wellbeing industry or if you're in an industry that relies on a person being motivated to take action.

For example, if you're selling some kind of coaching programme where you're teaching people to do x, y and z to improve their life/business/relationship (or whatever it is you're trying to fix) but a person has poor self-esteem and they lack confidence, they'll understand and agree others can do it, but they can't.

This is a mindset issue because the dialogue they have with themselves is convincing them to stay in their comfort zone. Lack of confidence is quite difficult to address, but with the right messaging and approach, it's possible to get people on board with you.

A few questions you need to be asking yourself include:

- Does my product or service increase the person's confidence?
- How does it do that?
- Does it increase my prospect's self-worth and self-esteem?

Make sure your marketing articulates this clearly and convincingly because for someone who is suffering from a lack of self-confidence, your messaging is key in helping them make a buying decision.

All-Out (Achieved by Force of Will)

All-out means your prospect is either going to go for it or not. There's NO halfway house or middle ground which means they're using the force of their will to achieve a result. Good examples include triathletes and extreme sports.

This level of internal belief typically refers to high achievers, who are around 20% of the typical population[3]. And then out of that 20%, there are probably around 5% who are

---

[3] Hal Elrod, (2017), The Miracle Morning: The 6 Habits That Will Transform Your Life Before 8AM, John Murray Learning

considered the cream of the crop. These are the people at whom you're really aiming your messaging.

For example, let's say your product is a language course and you're claiming prospects can learn a new language within 30 days, but this requires complete immersion for 30 days (in other words, you're eating, breathing, sleeping the language for 30 days). Because of the very nature of your product, you're only ever going to appeal to a certain portion of the market since it requires people to have full commitment.

People who are lazy and unmotivated, people who say they have a lot of ambition but don't (they don't have the desire to want to make that change), would never purchase a product like this.

Coaching Experience – I Can Do It if Someone Guides Me

Coaching experience basically involves prospects being guided towards a particular result. They're basically willing to do it – just not on their own, and want to be guided through the process step by step. So if you have a product or service that's going to take someone from A to B in a guided fashion, your core message should hinge on things like:

- Support through the process
- Accountability
- Tracking and monitoring of results
- Group support
- Guaranteed results (if appropriate).

Personal trainers are a great example, since they start by making a plan of action with their clients, showing them what to eat, how to structure their workouts, which supplements to take etc. This internal belief is quite easy to overcome as long as you really impress upon the customer the level of support they will receive and HOW this will help them.

Potluck – Maybe if I Get Lucky

Potluck is when your prospect believes a certain result is achievable if they get lucky. A good example of this would be something like the lottery or betting and competitions. The entertainment industry is also a perfect example of potluck; you see one hit wonders all the time and a lot of that is down to people being in the right place at the right time with the right set of circumstances.

Now, as a business owner, your job is to move people from complete scepticism to a believer (you will always find people at both ends of the spectrum). There will always be some people who never believe anything you say. These people are always the hardest to convert. On the other hand, some people will align with you perfectly and just want what you have; they don't need any convincing. And of course, there are also lots of people who fall in between.

Action Points

1. Look at each and every single product or service you're offering and ask yourself the following:

- Where does my product sit in comparison to the market?
- What claims am I making?
- What am I actually asking my prospects to do?
- Am I expecting my prospects to jump through hoops to attain a particular result?
- Can I give them guidance or coaching?
- Are my marketing campaigns speaking to my prospects' desires or am I speaking to ambition?
- Do my prospects struggle with a lack of confidence? If so, how can I change my messaging to help my prospects get around this issue?

2. List every single objection your prospects could potentially have in relation to your products/services. How can you overcome each objection?

External Belief Systems

External belief systems are the beliefs that are outside of a person, but to which they are affiliated and which heavily influence the way a person thinks, acts and behaves. Knowing about all of this is a key component of Mind-Hack™ Marketing. Without this knowledge, it can make the process of selling much more difficult.

For example, if you think about the way you conduct yourself on a day-to-day basis, you have your own set of thoughts and feelings. However, there's also a part of you affiliated to something else – like a movement, a key person of influence or even cultural, religious and societal norms. In other words, there's something you believe in (sometimes very strongly) which you hold in high esteem.

It's important to note that while you can overcome internal beliefs with great messaging, external belief systems are much harder to overcome because they consist of a set of ideals that a person has probably been exposed to for a very long length of time. It's usually something your prospect holds a very deep and often unshakeable belief in. Here's the thing: trying to sway someone away from their viewpoint is notoriously difficult to do because it doesn't make them feel good. In fact, it makes them feel guilty and leaves them with an overall bad feeling.

Wikipedia[4] **defines guilt as:** *"A cognitive or an emotional*

---

[4] Available at: https://en.wikipedia.org/wiki/Guilt_(emotion), accessed August 2021

experience that occurs when a person believes or realises — accurately or not — that they have compromised their own standards of conduct or have violated universal moral standards and bear significant responsibility for that violation."

Guilt can really cause a visceral reaction in people because they feel their actions are a betrayal of their beliefs and, in some cases, a betrayal of others. Religion is a great example, because if someone firmly believes in God and they do something against their religion, the guilt can be huge and overwhelming.

In terms of marketing, it pays to be aware of the external beliefs your prospects hold; and where possible, leverage them to your advantage which can help you secure a sale. I've explained some of the most common belief systems below.

Religion

Religion is probably the strongest of all external belief systems, with many wars having been fought in the name of religion. If somebody is brought up in a particular religion and practises their faith, they will literally fight to the death to defend their beliefs. If you have a product or a service that fits into the category of religion, then you're actually onto a winner.

American entrepreneur Dave Ramsey is a great example. Dave helps people (through his products and services) get out of debt. He's also a staunch Christian and his beliefs around money and the systems he uses to help people are inspired by the Bible. Because of these beliefs, he enjoys massive success by helping his community solve a very real problem (debt and responsible money management) – but he also helps them please God in the process.

Dave's community believe in the biblical method, and also believe they're doing something that's pleasing to their Lord. Religion is central to Dave's marketing and, as a result, more than 10 million people have used his system to get out of debt and win with money.

Dave's audience is predominantly Christian, and they follow him because they believe he's helping them to win in both their religion and their money – and that's an incredible combination. What's interesting about Dave Ramsey is that his religious angle has also attracted non-Christians who also believe in God to follow his methods too. And of course, there are those who follow Dave because his methods make sense – not because they believe in religion.

Your market is going to be the same as well – there will always be a very small percentage of people who don't really fit the norm of those you serve, and that's perfectly ok.

Politics

Politics is huge! If we take the example of the 2017 American Presidential Election, it was very clear that people fell into two camps – Trump or Clinton. There was a very small percentage of people who fell in between. It was a highly divisive election, but that's the nature of politics. Regardless of which country you're in, politics can unfortunately create an "us" versus "them" mentality.

If you support a certain political party, it's almost hardwired within you to be part of it, so anything that moves you away from your beliefs is going to make you feel uncomfortable and cause internal conflict. And because of this, people feel confused and will often fail to make the right decisions.

If you have a product or a service that falls into a "political" category, you can either play on it and use it as a strength, or you just need to be aware of it and make sure you're not saying or doing anything that's going to make your prospects feel uncomfortable.

For example, just nine days after President Trump decided to close the US borders to refugees, Airbnb pushed an ad campaign that played during the Super Bowl to directly oppose the decision.

The ad showed people of different nationalities together with the strapline: "We believe no matter who you are, where you're from, who you love or who you worship, we all belong. The world is more beautiful the more you accept."

So while Airbnb is not a politically based brand, they used politics in their ad campaign to make a point. It worked extremely well, and the company received high praise from audiences across the globe.

Nationalism

Nationalism is very similar to politics but has more to do with having pride in your country or the place where you're from. This is why you see, for example, holiday-makers who go to various different holiday resorts within their own country and collect souvenirs. Yes, it's a reminder of the place they visited, but it also ties into feelings of nationalism. While no one really needs "another souvenir", people buy them because they want anything that reminds them of being a part of that country.

For example, the Brexit situation in the UK highlighted the fact that people very firmly fell into either remaining in the EU or leaving it. While this does link to political beliefs, nationalism plays a much bigger part. Such strongly held beliefs are polarising and can create an "us versus them" mentality.

When it comes to your products and services, this can be very helpful as you can actually ensure your marketing and messaging speaks to the right people and the things they're most interested in. It can also spectacularly backfire.

A good example is the SodaStream brand. Based in Israel, the company has faced intense backlash because one of their plants is built on the West Bank. Further, actress Scarlett Johansson stepped down from her role as Oxfam ambassador after the charity strongly criticised her decision to spearhead the SodaStream ad campaigns.

When it comes to politics, religion and nationalism, be careful how you use these belief systems, since it can help or hinder your business.

Culture

Culture refers to the ideas, customs and social behaviour of a particular people or society and can really shape the way people think and buy. Culture is often geographically confined (but not always) or associated with a particular place.

For example, if you were living in a very conservative country where modesty is the considered norm and you decided to open a fashion boutique that offered something completely different to what's culturally acceptable, you'd almost definitely encounter resistance or even backlash. The likelihood of you having a successful business would be slim at best.

You might even damage your company name/brand if you're perceived as being culturally insensitive and lacking the respect and values that are important to local customs. For example, if you do business in the Middle East, it's not culturally acceptable to shake a woman's hand if you're a man. In some cases, it's seen as highly offensive. Not accepting food can also be seen as offensive in the Middle East, since the culture dictates that you should be hospitable at all times.

Community and Social Norms

Community and social norms are closely tied to culture, but have more to do with smaller, localised communities like villages, small towns and inner-city areas. This really comes down to being aware of your surroundings and is especially applicable if you have a bricks-and-mortar business. If you're selling something that goes against community and social norms, you're likely to face a lot of resistance.

For example, if you opened a nightclub in a quiet, conservative town, you might face criticism or even protests because you could be perceived as causing trouble or breaching the peace of the community.

Sometimes, a product or service doesn't have to be controversial to run into problems. A perfect example is if you opened a high-end luxury store in an area where poverty is common. You wouldn't have customers because most people wouldn't be able to afford you!

Key People of Influence

Key people of influence are people who are very well known and shape the world's opinions in any given field because they are considered to be the foremost experts in their field.

Tony Robbins and Brendon Burchard are good examples of key influencers in the personal development space. They have real influence on their followers who will pay tens of thousands of dollars or more just to hear them speak.

Richard Dawkins is another classic example. He falls under the category of religion in the sense that he doesn't have one since he's a die-hard atheist.

Key people of influence include experts, authority figures, social media influencers, thought leaders and idols. Some people think they are one and the same – but actually, they're not.

An *idol* is someone who is greatly loved and admired – like a pop star or celebrity. They have a cult-like following in the sense that they can almost do no wrong. Idols are almost worshipped to the point where some people can develop an unhealthy obsession with them, which is why they're called idols.

A good example of this is Justin Bieber; his fans go completely crazy over him and have been known to cry and faint at his concerts. People can get hysterical when it comes to their idols and will defend them even if they're in the wrong.

Experts are those who have expertise in their field but aren't necessarily well known – great examples are doctors and lawyers. In the celebrity world, experts are also people who have influence, such as Jillian Michaels and Dr Oz.

Authority figures are experts in one particular field who've authored a book – the clue of course is in the name. Anyone can write a book, but not all authors end up becoming key people of influence.

Social media influencers are as the name suggests – they have a following and impact and they influence their followers. They use *social* media to reach their followers and have established credibility in a specific industry. They can persuade followers to take action (such as to buy things) due to their trust and reach.

Take Huda Beauty as an example. Huda Kattan is the number one beauty blogger on the planet and started out on Instagram and YouTube. As of August 2021, she has over 49 million followers on Instagram which she used to launch her cosmetics line Huda Beauty. She has a net worth of over $510 million thanks to her followers who literally snap up everything she creates.

Thought leaders have a proprietary system or method to help their audience achieve a particular result. Thought leaders combine expertise, credibility and authority and a following; they're able to influence and persuade others. Great examples are Daniel Priestley, Simon Sinek, Dave Ramsey and Seth Godin.

All of the above have one thing in common: they're well known for what they do – and people with similar beliefs and values will align themselves with them. Getting a key influencer to endorse your products or services can literally create a surge in sales overnight.

Getting the right person of influence is about understanding who your audience is and where their beliefs sit. It's vitally important you don't get on the wrong side of these belief systems as this can really damage your brand, your reputation and your sales.

Combining the right key person of influence with an external belief system and an internal belief system can really skyrocket your results. Again, Dave Ramsey is an amazing example of this. He is someone who went through bankruptcy, was deeply in debt and then built his way to a $55 million fortune. His audience are predominantly Christian, struggling with debt and they look to Dave to help them out of their money problems.

Of all the external belief systems we've talked about so far, religion is by far the strongest. People live and die by their faith and will do their best not to do anything that would be against their religious code of conduct.

As a business, it pays to know your audience, and, where appropriate, accommodating beliefs can really help your sales. The fashion industry is a prime example of accommodating faith – specifically with the rise in modest fashion for faith-conscious Muslim women who want to wear beautiful clothes without having to worry about plunging necklines and short sleeves.

Brands such as H&M, ASOS and DKNY have both added modest fashion lines to their clothing ranges, and companies such as Dior and Yves Saint Laurent have their own range of modest clothing available exclusively in the Middle East. Smart? Definitely!

Now you may be thinking that your product or service isn't associated with a belief system, but that's not the point. Perhaps you've got a certain subset of people who use your product or service and maybe there's a way of serving their needs better.

For example, I know a very good dentist in the UK who has a lot of patients from the Middle East visit his practice for cosmetic procedures. They're mostly Muslim women who cover themselves from head to toe. And so, for them, he ensures all treatments are carried out by a female practitioner because he knows this will help them feel more comfortable. He's figured out how to give a subset of his customers what they really want without offending them and, because of this, has built a great reputation with his clients.

Clients literally fly in by the dozen just to visit his practice. It's really about understanding who the people you're serving are and how you can be sensitive to their needs.

Action Points
- Write down the core beliefs that would influence your prospect in relation to your product or service.
- How would this affect your prospect?
- How would it make them feel?

In addition to these action points, I highly recommend you complete the questions below. I've included answers for a fitness and weight loss plan as an example for you:

1. What does your prospect need to believe about YOU before they buy from you?

Prospects need to believe you have the experience, credentials and that you're the only expert who can specifically help them with their weight loss goals.

2. What does your prospect need to believe about themselves before they buy from you?

Prospects might have tried and failed at other plans before, therefore, they need to believe they have the will, the time and the determination to stick to the plan and get results. They don't need special equipment or to follow complex plans which might derail them.

3. What does your prospect need to believe about your product before they buy from you?

Prospects may have tried other products before, so they need to believe this is the only plan they need in order to succeed because it's easy to follow and gets results quickly.

A great marketer can easily satisfy all levels of belief in order to help the sale and move people from no to yes. If you're using email marketing, then you can easily turn each of these beliefs into a separate email, or even address them in one email right before you ask people to buy from you.

My favourite place to use these emails is as a cart-abandon sequence because, clearly, the customer is interested in your offers, but something is holding them back from buying. Your job is to ensure you've given them ALL the information they need to come to a buying decision.

Summary

In this chapter, we covered belief systems and how these impact your prospects' buying behaviour.

Specifically, we saw that:

- Internal belief systems are the deeper, more intrinsic reasons why someone buys, and are heavily influenced by thoughts and feelings.
- External belief systems include religion, politics, culture, influencers and other external factors that can shape and influence how someone thinks, acts and feels.
- There are varying levels of belief that can influence buying behaviour.
- Ignoring belief systems can have a negative impact on your business.

In the next chapter, we're going to dive even deeper into something that probably impacts buying behaviour more than anything else – identity and feelings.

Chapter 3: Identity and Feelings

In this chapter, we're going to explore your prospects' identity, their status, how they feel and how this impacts and influences buying behaviour. A key component in the Mind-Hack™ Method, identity and feelings have the deepest impact on a person's behaviour, more than anything else.

An *emotion* is a physiological experience or awareness that gives you information about the world. *Feelings* refer to the conscious awareness of the emotion itself. In short, it's the difference between having and knowing. The two are intrinsically linked and can hugely impact your identity.

Your *identity* is how you view yourself. The Oxford English Dictionary defines it as: *"The perception or recognition of one's characteristics as a particular individual, especially in relation to social context."*

Status refers to a person's condition, position or standing relative to that of others (for example, in society or among social circles).

Status and identity seem, at first glance, to be the same. However, a good distinction is that identity is intrinsic (how you view yourself), while status is extrinsic (how others view you).

In terms of marketing, here's the key point you need to remember: people will buy things that align with their identity or help them feel what they most desire. In other words, a person's buying decisions help to shape their identity (or at least they THINK these decisions help to shape their identity).

How Things Make You Feel

If I asked you to describe what kind of brand Apple is, you would probably say it's quite a cool, edgy and innovative brand. But how does that relate to a person?

Well, using Apple products (and being seen with them) might make a person feel cool and "on trend" – and there are other feelings that are associated with that, such as feeling successful (because Apple products aren't cheap!) and feeling as if you're ahead of the competition. Whether or not that's actually the case is another matter entirely – what matters is the person FEELS it.

However, it's not only to do with how a person is feeling, but also what a person is aspiring to be. This is one of the reasons why, for example, broke people buy luxury items which they can't actually afford. In fact, they get themselves into debt trying to buy these items because they want to feel cool and successful i.e. it's something they aspire to, but because they haven't yet succeeded, they'll buy products that reinforce that self-image instead.

This is HUGE! Identity is a massive reason why people buy. People always want to be a better version of themselves, and if you understand this on a deeper level and articulate this in your marketing, it will truly transform the way you do business.

Identity and feelings include things such as:

- Cool/boring
- Safety/fear
- Success/failure
- Confident/insecure
- In control/out of control
- Wealthy/broke

Your job as a business is to move people from a negative state to a positive state. For example, if somebody feels like a failure but your product or service helps them feel more successful, you're going to sell more of your product. If somebody is feeling insecure about their weight and appearance but you're helping them to feel more beautiful and confident, you're going to see sales increase, and so on.

Think about what your products and services can do for your prospects. Can your products help them go from boring to cool for example? Can you help a person feel safer, more confident or can you remove their self-doubt? If a person feels that using your product or services is going to improve their image or identity, they'll want to buy from you.

The Power of Social Influence on Identity

A while back, a gas heating engineer was checking my boiler and we had a candid conversation about business and cars. He told me that he recently bought a BMW 3 Series automatic – even though he only made £12,000 a year or £1,000 a month. Something didn't add up, because he was spending HALF of his salary on a car!

He certainly couldn't afford his car, but had justified the cost in his mind by convincing himself it was reliable and would "go at least 200,000 miles before it needed any serious maintenance."

Cars are a classic example of people buying on emotion and justifying with logic. A luxury car is one of the ultimate status symbols. An article published on inews.co.uk entitled "Social media driving millennials to buy cars they can't afford"[5] said that:

"More than half of young motorists say they feel pressured into buying a specific car to gain social status even if it means stretching their finances. A shocking 53 per cent of millennials said they had bought a car for status or prestige, with many citing influences from Facebook and Instagram as playing a part in their decisions."

The findings were drawn from research carried out by Admiral Loans who found that social influence and perception of others were hugely impactful on buying decisions. In a nutshell, people were buying cars they couldn't afford, with money they didn't really have, just to look good.

---

[5] Matt Allen, "Social media driving millennials to buy cars they can't afford", iNews, 27 August 2018, available at: https://inews.co.uk/essentials/lifestyle/cars/car-news/social-media-driving-millennials-to-buy-cars-they-cant-afford-191051

Emotions vs Logic

Back in 1983, Steve Jobs made a bold and daring move to sell his $10,000 computer "LISA" – he took out a nine-page advert in a national paper, selling the features of why his computer was amazing...

And the ad failed. Spectacularly.

It cost him an arm and a leg AND got him kicked off the project!

Why did it fail? Because Steve Jobs didn't understand the need to fulfil a really deep human need for emotion and the magic of, "What's in it for me?"

In other words, he made two critical mistakes in the ad: he talked relentlessly about the technical aspects and features of his product, AND he failed to talk about HOW the computer would change people's lives for the better.

It was cold. It was clinical. It was unrelatable and people didn't get it.

People don't always buy things just because of the obvious material benefits of having that thing, but because of a deeper, more intrinsic need.

Often, they want to feel better about themselves or they want to support or change their identity, or portray a certain image to others. They're basically buying the end results the product can give them.

So you're not buying a sports car, you're buying speed, and a product to raise your status in terms of feeling successful, wealthy and desirable.

In short, people want to feel good.

Going back to Steve Jobs, he learned a LOT from his epic failure and went and spent time with Disney Pixar's studio and learned the art of storytelling and emotions and how they relate to the end user.

He then took what he learned and applied this to everything Apple created after that.

Jobs came up with the slogan "Think Different" which fuelled the success of Apple and everything it did from that point onwards.

When Steve Jobs introduced the iPod, he didn't talk about it being 8GB or however much the data capacity was, rather he talked in terms of benefits and what these could do for you.

"1,000 songs in your pocket" replaced the previous boring and logical facts every other computing business was using.

Same thing, different perspective but MASSIVE difference in results.

Let's face it, unless you're a computer geek, you just can't relate to "8GB" because what the heck does that mean anyway??

1,000 songs in your pocket, on the other hand, is totally relatable. Everyone knows what that means – hours and hours of listening pleasure all on one neat little device... and sales EXPLODED.

If you want to see the original ad for this, go to YouTube and search for "First iPod Commercial 2001".

While the rest of the computing world was talking in GB and RAM and other technical (logical) jargon, Apple played on benefits and emotions and made their products cool, innovative and easy to understand.

And that's how they've now become the world's most successful company. Their entire brand is built on the philosophy of "Think Different".

So, how can you take this and apply it to your own business... and is there a secret formula for copy that converts more effectively and makes more sales?

There is.

It's called EMOTION.

Specifically, it's in a formula like this:

F + A + B + B + E = More Sales

And this, my friends, is where the secret formula comes in for how to write great copy that sells.

Here's what this all means:

F stands for Features – Features describe what a particular product has or does. So if a computer has 1TB, it describes how much data the computer is capable of holding.

A stands for Advantage – What advantage does a particular feature have over another? So a 1TB computer holds twice as much data as other models on the market. Advantages are always in relation to something else and great to include when your product is superior to your competitors' products, or even in relation to other products you sell.

B stands for Benefit – What are the core benefits of the product? For example, a 1TB computer can hold the equivalent of 100,000 files or however many that holds.

Notice in the formula I have B written twice – that's because we want to layer benefits or stack them by mentioning a benefit of a benefit.

So if my computer can hold 100,000 files, it will serve me for years to come without me having to upgrade my computer for more storage. See how that works?

E stands for Emotion – What's the core emotional need that the benefit fills for the customer? So if I don't need to upgrade my computer anytime soon, I don't need to worry or stress about running out of space anytime soon. In oth words, it puts me, the buyer, at ease in making my decision and helps to affirm it.

In fact, if you don't remember anything else, always remember this:

People buy on emotion and justify their buying decisions with logic.

This is exactly why you need both the benefits and the features of your products to make your marketing more effective. Benefits help to satisfy a person's emotional need to be better in some way, while features appeal to the logical side of a person's buying decision.

Feelings are powerful drivers for doing almost everything – from the choices we make on a daily basis, to life decisions and the people we choose to hang out with...

And it's NO different when it comes to selling.

If you sell weight loss products, what you're REALLY selling is the ability to make someone FEEL confident, attractive, healthy, sexy etc.

If you sell luxury cars, you're helping someone FEEL successful, powerful, in control and feel as if they've made it. This, of course, ties into the concept of identity and status which is driven from a deeper emotional need to be a better version of yourself. In short, it's about how you make someone feel.

In fact, as a rule (and as the writer Maya Angelou once said), people will forget what you said or did, but they'll never forget how you made them feel. The same is true for your market. You want your market to FEEL good about themselves. You want people to have an amazing experience buying from you – because that makes a person feel good.

Emotions are massive drivers and should NEVER be ignored in your marketing campaigns. Think about that carefully – why do people go out and do bad things? Because it makes them feel a certain way. Why do people do selfless acts? Because it feels rewarding and gives YOU the pleasure of helping someone out. It's ALLLLL about you!

Most of the big brands get it – but sadly, smaller businesses that struggle with their marketing messages usually trip up by talking about how cool they are and how amazing their product is; they fail to talk about what the product or service will DO to change the person's life.

So just like Steve Jobs did with his computer LISA, most businesses talk features with the odd benefit thrown in.

Successful businesses focus on the benefits for their audience… while super-successful businesses create maximum impact by talking about emotions and feelings and, more importantly, how those emotions and feelings make a person feel better about themselves.

By only talking about features and technical information, you're leaving money on the table.

To help you fix this problem, complete the exercise below.

Action Points

1. List all the possible features of your product or service.
2. Write down the benefits of each particular feature.
3. Write down the benefits of each particular benefit and keep going until you can go no further.
4. Use your benefits in your copy wherever possible!

Example:

A face cream might contain SPF30 which is a feature, but the benefit is it protects your skin from the sun.

So instead of saying, "Contains SPF30", you now say, *"SPF30 defends skin against the sun's harmful rays."* This will give you a basic benefit-driven description... but we don't want basic – we want powerful!

Now layer the description with a "benefit of the benefit" and this time make it emotionally driven. I like to use the connecting phrase "so that" or "which will" as follows: *"SPF30 defends skin against the sun's harmful rays* **so that** *you can look and feel younger for longer."*

Now this sounds WAY more powerful and compelling than simply saying, "Contains SPF30" or, "SPF30 defends skin against the sun's harmful rays."

Do this with all your marketing messages — taking each feature you mention and turning them into emotionally driven benefits. Just this one aspect of your marketing will help you sell more of your products and services.

It's a fantastic and easy place to start and WILL get you more powerful results in your campaigns.

Summary

In this chapter, we talked at length about how a person's identity and feelings impact their buying behaviour and choices.

The key takeaways from this chapter are:

- Identity and status impact buying decisions in a very profound way because people always want to be a better version of themselves.
- It's your job as a business to articulate the transformation people will get from your products or services.
- People buy on emotion and justify their buying decisions with logic – which is why effective marketing campaigns include both.

In the next chapter, we'll start digging deep into your ideal customer or avatar. Specifically, we're going to explore the customer journey and how you can use this to help more of your prospects become paying customers.

Chapter 4: Mapping Out the Customer Journey

I often get asked to create effective marketing campaigns for businesses in tough markets. One of my clients is in the "high-ticket sales" space – a saturated market that is overflowing with salespeople all claiming they're the best at what they do.

Despite how saturated the market is, the sales funnel I created for my client had a consistent average email-open rate of 54%. For yet another one of my clients (a medical doctor serving other doctors in a tough niche), the campaign I created for him had an average email-open rate of 73%.

How was this possible? Because I understood two critical things: who the ideal avatar is, and what the customer journey is. These examples show you the power of Mind-Hack™ Marketing in action.

The customer journey is the process by which prospects/ customers interact with your business in order to achieve a particular goal.

Understanding this process is going to help you become better at marketing and better at creating a great experience for your audience – which ultimately will result in more sales.

That's why in this chapter, we'll explore the customer journey and how to map this out for your business.

Understanding the Customer Journey

Many people confuse the customer journey with a sales funnel and falsely assume the two are the same thing.

The main difference between a customer journey and a sales funnel is that the customer journey is a representation of the entire overall path a person takes, from interest all the way to making a purchase. A sales funnel, however, is the specific process of turning visitors into leads and leads into customers.

For example, before someone purchases from you, they may have completed the following actions:

- Read a blog post
- Engaged with your social media posts
- Watched a YouTube video
- Joined your Facebook group
- Watched Facebook Lives
- Listened to a podcast
- Seen one of your ads
- Opted into your list
- Read Google reviews
- Engaged with your emails...

And not necessarily in that order!

We'll talk more about sales funnels later in the book, but the key thing you need to understand is that the customer journey involves multiple touchpoints with prospects and

customers.

An effective marketing campaign means first understanding what this journey looks like for a potential customer, and then optimising it so that it fully supports the natural progression from a visitor to a lead, and then from a lead to a customer and a repeat customer.

Unfortunately, many businesses think the customer journey is restricted to one set of touchpoints, without really considering the fact that a prospect can enter your world from any touchpoint.

Sometimes, a customer may well bypass ALL touchpoints and come straight to you through a referral. It may sound complicated, but actually, the only thing you need to be aware of is that ANYONE can enter your world at ANY point.

Your job as a business owner is to create a great customer experience regardless of how someone interacts with your brand. The difference between a good customer experience and an exceptional one really does come down to the details and the quality of each interaction they have with your business.

By mapping out the customer journey, it helps you understand the high-level overview of how your audience is finding you and interacting with you. The aim is to figure out how you can optimise or engineer each interaction and experience, so it helps your audience want to take the next step with your business.

Mapping the customer journey always starts with understanding your ideal customer and what they want – and then figuring out the best ways to help them make an empowered buying decision with the right information.

The other major benefit of mapping the customer journey carefully is you can clearly see where the gaps are and what needs to be improved and where.

Google's Zero Moment of Truth

During the customer journey, there is a point where the prospect is ready to become a customer. Google calls this the "zero moment of truth" or ZMOT – it refers to the moment in the buying cycle when the prospect researches a product just before they decide to buy.

Typically, before someone makes a buying decision, they might do any of the following:

- Check your reviews online.
- Check testimonials and case studies.
- Look at competitor products.
- Speak to friends.

In other words, the decision between wanting something and actually buying is not a linear decision. Your job is to make the customer journey as easy and as frictionless as possible, giving prospects what they need in order to progress to a paying customer.

The number of touchpoints is extremely important in the customer journey – and varies depending on which industry you fall under.

In fact, it can be anywhere between seven and 22 touchpoints BEFORE prospects decide to buy!

In business to business (B2B) markets, buyers typically consume 13 pieces of content BEFORE making a buying decision, whereas for business to consumer markets (B2C), it can vary between 10 and even 40 depending on the product.

In short, prospects want to:

- Compare your product to alternatives.
- Check reviews and mentions on social media.
- See examples/applications of your product in use.

So what does this mean for you?

Simply put, there are a few things you can do to improve your chances of prospects becoming buyers:

- Provide regular awesome content that solves problems for your ideal customers.
- Encourage customers to leave reviews on Google, your website, social media etc.
- Ask for video testimonials of your products/services.
- Find ways to engage with potential customers through social media, email and more premium content people have to sign up for.

Exercise: How Do I Map My Customer Journey?

The following exercise will help you think about the customer journey in a lot more detail. A simple spreadsheet is a great way to capture this information:

Step 1 - Create Awareness:
- What can you do to get in front of your ideal customers?
- Which social media platforms can you hang out on and what kind of content can you create that solves the problems your audience is interested in?
- What kind of ads can you run to get people excited about what you have to offer?

Step 2 - Create Engagement:
- How can you get people to engage with your brand?
- Can you engage them on social media and get people into a Facebook group or encourage them to comment/regularly consume your free information?
- Can you poll/survey/quiz your audience?
- Which medium does your audience

prefer? Do they prefer video, reading or listening or a combination of both? If you get this wrong, your audience will never consume your message!

Step 3 - Hook Them In:
- What can you offer of value in exchange for your prospect's email address?
- Write at LEAST seven emails in your funnel to get people excited, solve problems and offer your best content to get prospects hooked!
- Ensure your free content has a call to action at the end to turn visitors into actual subscribers.
- Can you create several pieces of content that people can sign up for that solves different problems?

Step 4 - Sell to Them:
- At this stage, encourage prospects to become paying customers.
- What can you offer that's low cost and low risk, but super-high value?
- If you've used paid advertising, your goal is to at least cover the cost of your ad spend.

Step 5 - Create an Exceptional Experience:
- Nothing makes a new customer happier than feeling as if the vendor has gone above and beyond in creating a fantastic experience.
- Give surprise bonuses, make customer service easy, send even more helpful content so customers feel excited and wowed.
- What can you offer/do/create to ensure an exceptional experience?

Step 6 - Create Loyalty:
- Creating a customer isn't enough. You want customers to buy from you repeatedly.
- What can you offer to ascend customers to another level?
- Can you offer a VIP service, more bells and whistles, done for you etc.?
- Where are the opportunities to offer customers additional products and services?
- What are customers asking for that you don't currently sell but could?

Step 7 - Ask for Reviews:

- Happy customers love to share their experiences!
- Ask them to leave reviews on Google/ your website/social media.
- Ask for testimonials so other prospects can make an empowered buying decision too.

Step 8 - Create Raving Fans:

- Raving fans actively tell the world about how awesome you are and will gladly refer you to others.
- Can you create a process for actively asking for referrals?
- Could you offer an affiliate/partner programme?

Hopefully you can see from this exercise that multiple touchpoints for your audience are a must, and that your job is to make each stage of this journey as easy and as value packed as possible.

The key thing to remember is the word EASY – customers LOVE easy. Therefore, make every interaction easy and make the change between each stage in the customer journey as easy and as frictionless as possible.

If you need help with customer journey mapping, simply go to my website to learn more: http://arfasairaiqbal.com/mindhackresources.

Avatars vs Personas

Your *avatar* is a general description of the kind of person, with an underlying problem they need resolving, who will buy your product or service. So for example, if you offer a weight loss product, a busy career woman who wants to lose weight might be your general avatar.

Personas are a subset of your avatar and represent a narrowed segment of the market. So, if your general avatar is a busy career woman who's looking to lose weight, one of the personas could be a woman who is about to get married. Her needs are going to be a little bit different because she is up against a deadline and has the goal of getting into her wedding dress. She would be looking to drop weight very quickly.

Another persona could be a woman who has just given birth. Because she is taking care of a baby, she is going to ep deprived and very pressed for time. She may also sing her child so her nutritional needs are going to be very different. While she still wants to lose weight and look her best, she has a different set of challenges.

Personas allow you to create more specific sales messages, because the more specific you get, the more you will emotionally connect and resonate with your prospect. So your first task is to identify who your personas are before you flesh out the details.

When creating your marketing campaigns, the idea is to use all of the information you've gathered previously and write a very detailed description of your avatar and personas. As you write a detailed account of your ideal prospect, you really want to be thinking about their day-to-day struggles, their needs and desires. Give your avatar a name and get specific with how you build out your avatar.

Think about your avatar and personas (I'll refer to both of these as "avatars" in this book because it's easier!) as a real person, because when you create your campaigns, you'll write to your avatars. This will ensure the messages are highly relevant to your ideal prospect and will leave them feeling as if you're specifically speaking to them. This specificity helps you build connection with your audience.

At this point, some of my clients usually wonder if there's such a thing as too many avatars, and the answer is NO. One client that I worked with had eight different personas and anyone who fell outside of those personas was classified as being under the general avatar. Based on this, I created an email campaign for each persona, plus a more general avatar email campaign.

It took a good few months to put the campaigns together because by the time I had finished, we had over 100 emails. Was it worth it? Well, thanks to the new segmentation, we saw a huge boost in sales within the first six weeks.

There was no additional marketing spend or awareness activities taking place; the only change to the entire business was the introduction of the persona-specific and general avatar email campaigns. Having both meant that we could specifically target the eight personas as well as catching anyone who didn't fit into them – no one was missed and everyone received something better targeted to them.

Over a period of eight weeks, we saw the full effects of the campaign. An additional £1,800–£2,000 of sales per month, every month like clockwork! For a small business selling £14-a-month memberships, this was a serious breakthrough in revenue which dramatically turned the business around.

So, over to you now. Write down a DETAILED account of your ideal prospect and their day-to-day struggles and wants. Name your avatar and be specific with your details.

Here's an example avatar below for a weight loss product:

Prospect Avatar: Busy Career Woman Who Needs to Lose Weight

Kim is a 34-year-old woman who has a steady desk job and a quiet social life. She is single and has been for some time. Kim is a great person to be around and is the life and soul of any party. However, Kim is shy around men and very withdrawn. She is a size 16 and can't wear the high-fashion clothes her friends do.

Kim tends to hide behind dull, baggy clothes in an attempt to hide her body and blend into the background. She is comfortable around friends and people she knows, but not around strangers. She recently passed up on the opportunity to get a promotion from assistant consultant to a consultant at a local IT firm because she lacked the confidence to apply for the job. She genuinely thought she wasn't smart enough to fit into the role.

Kim never works out. Long hours at the office and helping to care for her arthritic mother at home often mean Kim is too busy to cook healthy meals or do workouts. She usually enjoys takeaway food and has found she is only getting heavier and more out of shape as the months go by.

Kim would love to look glamorous and fancies a guy at work. She has been friends with him for a long time but doesn't have the confidence to ask him out because she doesn't feel she is good enough. Kim rarely chooses to go out to parties where there are a lot of men, simply because she finds the prospect of being noticed too much. She secretly wants to be noticed, but because she hates her body, she prefers to avoid situations where she thinks she will be noticed.

Kim is worried her age is against her – most of her friends are either married or have a partner and are happy and settled. She is also worried that her biological clock is ticking. She would love to meet the man of her dreams, get married and have kids. However, because she is so shy and dislikes her appearance so much, she chooses to ignore what she really wants because she truly believes it can't happen.

Kim has tried many diets and failed. Her weight has been an issue throughout her whole life and now she has been told she is at risk of diabetes if she doesn't lose some serious weight. Her office party is coming up at Christmas and Kim has two months to go. For the first time in her life, Kim wants to make an effort and look good and ask her colleague out on a date. She has heard rumours that her colleague will be moving to another office out of town in the new year and Kim really wants to impress before he leaves. She needs a total solution to her problems right now.

Pretty detailed, right? I agree this takes time; however, the results are well worth the time invested in this task. It's precisely this level of detail that will help you get your campaigns right. Once you've done this with your avatar, you want to do the exact same exercise again, but this time for your personas.

I run a two-day workshop on building out your avatars where you'll do a super-deep dive into the entire Mind-Hack™ Marketing process. To find out more, please go to: http://arfasairaiqbal.com/mindhackresources.

Negative Avatars

Several years ago, when I was new in business, I took on a business partner – a fellow copywriter who shared the same vision as me (or so I thought!). A few weeks into the new partnership, there was trouble in paradise...

What I initially thought of as a good idea turned sour very quickly...

Late on delivering work, a poor work ethos, constant hand-holding and just being plain difficult, my so-called business partner had excuses for everything.

Unfortunately, I put up with him for way longer than I needed to, but the straw that finally broke the camel's back was when I paid him to do some work for me. Not only did he deliver a fraction of what I asked for, the work itself was substandard.

I was fuming!

To top it all off, clients started complaining about his bad attitude and another copywriter wrote me a very strongly worded email urging me to "seriously reconsider" my business partner.

So I had to let him go and I fired him in the nicest way possible...

And rather than take responsibility for his behaviour, he chose to retaliate with bad language and personal insults instead (no surprises there!).

Anyway, there's a very good reason why I'm sharing this with you and it's this:

Defining who you hire or choose to work with is critical to the growth of your business.

A key takeaway from my experience (and a big lesson for your business) is that credentials aren't everything.

In fact, I would argue that credentials are SECONDARY when hiring or working with someone, because WHO you hire is more important than what you think you are hiring.

Ultimately, when it comes to making money in your business, it's not just about finding the right customer... **it's also about finding the right fit for your team!**

The wrong person on your team can sap your energy, reduce productivity and create all sorts of problems for you and your business – and this can deeply impact your profitability.

In hindsight, my ex-business partner is the perfect example of a "negative avatar".

A negative avatar is the exact opposite of your perfect avatar – and it's something you need to pay very careful attention to in your business or you'll end up dealing with people like my ex-business partner!

Had I understood my avatar and negative avatar properly, I would have made a better hiring decision.

But it's not JUST hiring and partnerships that are affected by not knowing your ideal avatar and negative avatar.

It's also about the quality of the leads you generate for your business.

Several years ago, I went through a period of intense stress when I was going through my divorce, and my health took a nosedive...

I wasn't sleeping, felt totally drained and developed sudden allergies to foods I'd previously eaten my whole life. Even breakfast cereal would cause me to break out in severe hives.

At the time, I was completely broke, and so when I found a food allergy test being sold on a famous deal site, I bought it straight away and booked onto a consultation.

I arrived a few days later at a small clinic where my practitioner went through a number of allergy tests with me.

At the end of my assessment, my practitioner made some very expensive recommendations for me which I couldn't possibly manage – so I had to politely decline. We got talking about deal sites and I asked him whether this form of marketing was working in his business.

Sadly, despite having hundreds of people turn up for a food

allergy test, *not a single person had bought anything beyond the initial assessment.*

Not only had he wasted hundreds of precious hours in testing people who never bought anything from him, he wasn't even able to book a single follow-up appointment!

The volume of leads wasn't the problem, they were just poorly qualified – and here's why:

While the practitioner was definitely providing a valuable service, his lead-generation strategy was completely flawed.

He had failed to understand his ideal customer and was therefore attracting his negative avatars instead.

Why?

Because the mindset of most people who typically go to deal sites is that of "instant gratification", "discounts" and "cheap deals"...

Meaning that such prospects would rarely convert into long-term customers. For the practitioner, any money made from the initial deal had to be split equally with the deal site, meaning the clinic made a loss from the campaign.

This is a perfect example of how cheap leads are not always best and can, in many instances, totally backfire on you.

While deal sites are just ONE example of the wrong kind

of leads for your business, there are so many others that business owners just like you deal with on a daily basis. But there IS a better way.

I'm a HUGE fan of pre-qualifying leads on your list, because every wrong lead means you're paying for the lead to be on your list.

Wrong leads don't buy from you. And they can't be convinced to "eventually" buy your stuff. It rarely happens.

And even if they DO buy from you, they rarely make good customers or clients because they'll complain, whinge and moan about everything!

Knowing who your negative avatar is will allow you to eliminate the tyre-kickers and freebie seekers in your business.

It also allows you to keep your list clean and ensures the quality of your list stays high. Your open and click-through rates from emails will be better. You'll sell more products and services. And you'll deal with less drama, fewer refunds and fewer complaints.

Action Points

Attracting the wrong kind of person in your business can literally cripple your profits because you've wasted your hard-earned cash on acquiring leads who'll give you more hassle than money... which is why defining your negative avatar is just as critical as your ideal avatar.

So here are a few things to consider when pulling together your campaigns:

- Define your negative avatar – write down everything that defines your idea of a nightmare customer and get really detailed about it.
- Give this avatar a name and an actual picture if possible.
- When writing your campaigns, ensure the language you use repels your negative avatar. For example, if you're selling a programme that takes real work and consistent effort, you can say, "This isn't for people who are looking for get-rich-quick schemes or who think they can achieve success without putting the effort in."

- Your first interactions with people should immediately repel the wrong people and attract the right ones.

The key to making this work properly is to refer to your negative avatar very sparingly – you want to focus overwhelmingly on your ideal avatar, but you should (where relevant) let your audience know who your product is not for.

Summary

The ideal customer journey is the process by which prospects/ customers interact with your business in order to achieve a particular goal.

The key takeaways from this chapter include:

- The ideal customer journey includes at least eight different steps, from initial awareness to creating a raving fan.
- Understanding this process will help you create a great experience for your audience.
- Done properly, the ideal customer journey will help you increase sales and profitability.
- Avatars represent your general market.
- Personas are a subset of your avatar and represent a

narrowed segment of the market.

- Medium is just as vital as your market and your message, but is often overlooked.
- If your campaign is tightly put together but still isn't converting, it may be that your medium is off.
- Negative avatars are important to identify because you want to ensure you don't attract the wrong person into your business.

Now you've understood how to map the customer journey, you may be wondering how to find more of your ideal customers.

That's what we'll be discussing in the next chapter, where you'll discover how to research your market effectively so you CAN find more of your ideal customers.

Chapter 5: Market Research

Market research is the key to understanding your market and crucial to the Mind-Hack™ Marketing process. It will help you gain an insight into the demographics of your audience so your message to market is accurate. Unless you know with 100% certainty who you are serving, never skip this crucial part of the process.

You have to remember that people are complicated creatures. And relationships are complicated too. Marketing is a relationship between you and your ideal customer (also known as your avatar). This is why a mixture of understanding your market and making best guesses about your avatar is the best way to create your campaigns.

Where possible, be as specific as you can in order to home in on your target market during your research. For example, the age of your audience might be between 20 and 35, and whilst there will be people that fall outside of this range, about 80% of your audience will fall within it. Your job is to focus on the majority.

So if your marketing is talking about issues that affect somebody who is older than this age range, people in your ideal age range are going to feel alienated because they feel it doesn't apply to them.

Market research helps you refine your marketing messages depending on the data you collect about your audience. It helps you identify your ideal customers and ensures your ad targeting on platforms such as Facebook is as accurate as possible.

In previous chapters, we've covered the area of psychographics and have already covered the reasons why people buy or don't buy, but now we want to focus on the **demographics of your ideal customer.**

Demographics refer to all of the data associated with your ideal customer e.g. age, gender, where they live, income level etc.

There are dozens of ways to research your target market, so in this chapter, we'll cover several different ways, including:

- Existing data
- Google Analytics
- Social media audience insights
- Survey your list
- Competitor analysis
- Google Search – blogs, sites, forums
- Alexa
- Ask the right questions
- Reverse engineer your product/service
- Social media habits.

While market research isn't exactly the most exciting task to do, the quality of your research can unlock a treasure chest of valuable information you might never have known existed.

It's worth spending a few hours of your time to do at least some basic research – but the more time you dedicate to it, the better the quality of the answers you will get, and the more they will help you with creating your marketing campaigns.

The key pieces of information you need to focus on in your research are things like age, gender, where they live, income level, marital status, education level, whether they're a homeowner, and buying habits etc.

You ALSO want to research the most common problems people are struggling with and what kind of outcome or results they are looking for. This is the kind of data most marketers focus on.

Data Gathering Techniques

Existing data is the most obvious place to start, since it's data you hold about your existing customers. Depending on what kind of industry you're in, you might have detailed data about your customers or you might only have their name and email. Detailed data requires the discipline of going through it carefully, trying to spot trends and building a snapshot of your audience.

If you don't have much data, consider adding an additional form after they sign up or give you their initial details, and ask for information such as age, gender and postcode. This is known as two-step sign-up and works well because it doesn't hinder the sign-up process. Once you have data, you can draw a lot of inferences from it.

For example, if you research postcodes, you can learn about the kind of homes in the area and the average house price, local amenities and income level. If you had a postcode area where all the houses were valued at around the half a million mark, assuming those people are wealthy and that they like the finer things in life would be logical.

An important point to note here is that you should provide a range of values (age, income) for your audience to select rather than ask for an absolute value. This will make the data easier to read and also is less intrusive for your audience than asking for specifics. Try to keep the order of the ranges small so that your data is more specific and you can make good inferences from it.

Google Analytics

Google Analytics is an incredibly rich source of information and, as long as your website has this properly set up, you can get lots of valuable insights into your website visitors. For example, referral traffic will show you where your website visitors are coming from, including whether the traffic is organic or from a paid source such as Google Ads. You'll be able to accurately see which social media platforms your visitors are coming from. You can even see which type of traffic is most likely to convert into sales.

Audience Insights

Audience Insights in Facebook is similar to Google Analytics because of the level of detailed data it can provide. You can gather data like interests, country, income level, if your audience are homeowners etc., which can then help you make inferences about your ideal customers.

So if your audience are homeowners for example, you can safely assume they probably have more money at their disposal than a non-homeowner. Facebook allows you to get incredibly granular with the level of detail available.

Pinterest is another great place for market research, since you can search just about anything you like in the same way you would on Google. Pinterest will show you key trends in a visual format and works especially well if you have a product-based business.

Surveys

Surveys are especially useful if you have an existing, engaged list. Depending on your industry, it's not always appropriate to ask people for their age and income details after sign-up. When sending out a survey to your list, it's important your audience understand why you are sending it to them.

Be transparent and tell them the following:

- You want to send them relevant and helpful information.
- You want to improve your products and services.

- You want to improve the customer experience.
- How long the survey will take.

As a general rule of thumb, the longer the survey, the smaller the percentage of people who are likely to fill it out. Keep your surveys as short and to the point as possible and ask only the most relevant questions you need to.

If you're offering a high-ticket product or service, or you're in an industry where your customers are very closely working with you, you're much more likely to get detailed responses to your surveys. Outside of this, text-based answers are going to be more rich and informative, but most people won't take their time to do that – so include questions with a small number of choices where they can tick a checkbox.

Offering an incentive like a discount, voucher code, bonus, free gift or free delivery etc. can increase your response rates. **Above all, the number one rule when it comes to surveys is to keep them simple!**

Don't make survey questions vague or overly complicated. Avoid using required fields because some people are lazy and can't be bothered to answer every question – therefore, they'll enter anything just because they have to! By making your survey questions optional, you'll make your answers MORE accurate than if you made your questions required.

Some questions you could ask include:

- What's your biggest challenge with (insert niche)?

- Where do you feel you're most stuck?
- What do you really need help with?
- What are your biggest objections in doing business with us?
- How do you prefer to learn?
- What do you want to achieve the most?

Remember, all of these questions should be optional and always in relation to the niche you're in or in relation to your product or service.

Tools like SurveyMonkey are incredibly simple to use both in terms of constructing the actual survey and gathering the data. Similar to surveying your list, you can run polls on Facebook which are actually a quick and easy way to gather feedback from your audience.

Podio (a project management tool) is a great platform to use for surveys as it gives you the ability to create a form with a weblink that you can add to emails and Facebook posts etc. You can then run reports on the survey responses, making this a really great tool to use.

Last but not least, Google Forms is a simple, easy and intuitive option for creating surveys and is also free to use.

Competitor Analysis

If you're really stuck and have no idea where to start, or you're starting out with a brand-new business and don't have any data, then competitor analysis is the best way of getting an insight into your market. You'd be shocked at the number of businesses that never bother to check their competitors properly!

Check your competitors' websites to get a feel for their brand and the way they communicate with their audience. Do one better and place an order from a competitor and see what kind of communications you get from them. In particular, look at all the emails you get with your order. Are you added to a welcome series? Do you get additional emails with tips on how to use your new purchase? If you bought a physical product, what kind of marketing materials were inside the package when it arrived?

Another fantastic resource is scouring the comments section of your competitors' social media accounts. What are people saying and how are your competitors responding to their comments?

What are their customers happy about and what are they complaining about? You can also find a wealth of information on the social media accounts of influencers in your industry.

What kind of things are people struggling with? What are they frustrated about? Which common themes keep cropping up in the comments?

You'll learn a TON from researching your competitors, and you can go one step deeper by checking the demographic information of the kind of people your competitors are attracting.

Some key actions you can take include:

- Listing all your competitors and outlining their offers. How are these different to what you are offering?
- What's their unique selling point (USP)?
- Where are they advertising?
- What kind of offers are they running in their ads?
- What kinds of content are they producing?
- What kind of engagement do their social media accounts have?
- What could you do better than they do?
- What could you do that your competitors can't?
- Check their reviews online – what are people praising them for? What are people complaining about?
- What kind of comments do their audience keep making?

Google-Searching Websites, Blogs and Forums

Another way you can carry out market research is via search engines like Google and Bing – use these to find relevant websites, blog sites, forums and associated social media sites in your industry.

Simply type in "the best (insert your niche/industry) blogs". You can replace blogs with websites, forums, podcasts, YouTube channels, books and even social media sites. Ideally, you should be Googling all of these and compiling a document or spreadsheet that records your findings.

What you're looking for are common themes, pain points and frustrations affecting your niche. Pay attention to the number of shares and likes on blog posts, how many people have watched or downloaded something or commented on a particular topic. This is GOLD DUST! You'll gain insights into your niche that you might never have even thought about.

Alexa and BuzzSumo

Other ways you can glean information are through sites like Alexa.com and BuzzSumo.com. These can give you incredible insights and information on key sites that are trending in your niche right now.

BuzzSumo in particular is a fantastic resource and will help you get crystal clear on the problems your niche is facing or the kinds of topics people in your niche are consuming.

Ask the Right Questions

Sometimes the best way to get information about your ideal audience is to ask them directly! Ask the right questions and find different ways to interact with your audience. If you have an email list and you have already surveyed them but you want to know more, think about asking questions on your social media pages – Facebook, Instagram and Twitter are all great places to ask questions.

One of my clients has a YouTube channel and he does the same thing: he asks his viewers questions and encourages them to reply in the comments – and they do. If people think you care enough about their problems and see you're willing to go out of your way to help them (by giving them valuable content), they will engage with you and they'll share their struggles and needs with you.

Reverse Engineering Your Product/Service

Another way of getting good information on your target market is to reverse engineer your product or service. Start by thinking about your product/service and ask yourself the following questions:

- Why did I create it?
- What need was I trying to fulfil?
- What kind of person would want my product or service?

A lot of business owners often create products or services based on their own struggle to find a satisfactory solution to a problem they have. Maybe you fall into that category, and if so, think about why you created your product or service – who were you aiming it at? What specific problem were you trying to solve? And then think about the types of people you would want to buy from you.

Very often, just by doing a little bit of analysis, you can actually come up with a lot of useful information that is really relevant for your marketing.

Social Media Habits

A general point that you might want to consider is that certain social media platforms are popular with certain demographics. For example, there are more men on Twitter than women[6], most probably because men in general tend to be more concise and speak less than women do.

It's also a platform that a lot of celebrities and thought leaders use to convey their message. Pinterest, on the other hand, is the opposite: almost 80% of its users are women[7], of which a large proportion are considered to be affluent or with a higher disposable income.

Facebook is a very generic platform and so you will see all sorts of demographics represented, from pensioners to Millennials and everything in between. Snapchat and Instagram are both very popular with Millennials and Generation Z. So again, you want to think about your target demographic and which social platforms they're going to be visiting.

Another important point to consider is the type of product and service you're selling in relation to social media preferences. So, if you're selling makeup or you're a makeup artist, Twitter won't be any good for you because it's not really a visual platform.

Instagram and Pinterest are going to be far better as they are image-led platforms. YouTube is also definitely a good platform to consider because people go there looking for how to do something.

---

[6] Salman Aslam, (2021), 'Twitter by the Numbers: Stats, Demographics & Fun Facts, Omnicore, 3 January, available at: https://www.omnicoreagency.com/twitter-statistics/
[7] Salman Aslam, (2021), 'Pinterest by the Numbers: Stats, Demographics & Fun Facts, Omnicore, 4 January, available at: https://www.omnicoreagency.com/pinterest-statistics/

Therefore, if you were a makeup artist, you would research the big beauty influencers who have channels on YouTube (which would be very useful for targeting purposes if they had a paid ad running on YouTube) or you may even set up your own YouTube channel to show makeup tutorials.

YouTube is amazing for research because, at the time of writing, it's officially the second largest search engine in the world after Google[8] – yet it's often overlooked by businesses for research.

Some bloggers and YouTubers have huge followings. There used to be a time when only celebrities and really famous people had a following and the kind of influence that could drive sales for a product they used.

However, it's no longer a privilege that's afforded only to celebrities. Now bloggers and vloggers (video bloggers) who've got a passion they want to share with the world amass huge followings. In some cases, they have the same level of influence as A-list actors, models and musicians.

Another very important point to consider when you're doing your research is to ask yourself whether your audience are watchers or readers. This is all about understanding the medium preferred by your audience so you know the right platform to advertise on. For example, let's say you sell women's jewellery, platforms like Instagram and Pinterest

[8] Dave Davies, (2021), 'Meet the 7 Most Popular Search Engines in the Wor Engine Journal, 3 March, available at: https://www.searchenginejournal.co meet-search-engines/#close

would work best for you.

However, if you were teaching people how to make jewellery, then YouTube would be perfect because your audience would want to watch tutorials rather than read books about how to make jewellery.

As a side note, Facebook tends to boost video views. The reason it does that is because Facebook prefers people to stay on its platform rather than clicking on a link and going to an external site like YouTube. This means Facebook favours video content that sits on its platform, which is great for sharing because it's most likely your ideal audience are on Facebook.

Another point to keep in mind regarding Facebook is that most people are on there just to catch up with friends in their network, to engage with others and to pass time. It's not really the place people go to read long posts, as most people would actually go to a separate website or blog to do that.

So you need to be careful if you've got a lead magnet that's like a big book or detailed guide about a topic related to your industry, because it may not work on Facebook. Of course there are always going to be exceptions to the rules, but these are just some things that you need to start thinking about – and making a note of during your research phase.

How Is This Research Relevant to Your Marketing?

ɔmetimes when you're in the thick of your research, it can

seem a little overwhelming and you might feel as if you're collecting data without really understanding how this is relevant to your marketing.

If we take the weight loss industry as an example, and you're selling vegan food, then your ideal customer or avatar is somebody who is into healthy eating and is a vegan. So maybe they watch something like Food Matters TV, which is dedicated to healthy eating and healthy living. They may follow people like Ella Woodward on YouTube and follow blogs such as Oh She Glows.

Similarly, as part of your research, you also need to consider the kind of goals, values, aspirations and dreams of your target audience. So, taking the weight loss industry as an example, you've got thought leaders like Jillian Michaels who has all sorts of products to help people achieve the body of their dreams.

However, if you watch her videos carefully, she has a very unique style and talks a LOT about motivation and really pushing yourself to be the best you can be. She is also known as "TV's toughest trainer" and because of her image and style, there's a certain type of person who is going to be following and watching those kinds of videos. She certainly wouldn't appeal to someone who is afraid of pushing themselves.

And again, it's just about being aware of all these factors when you're doing your research and creating your campaigns. The way you write your materials should be dictated by your avatar.

Action Points

Analyse your market carefully using the different methods outlined in this chapter and ask yourself the following questions about your market:

- What do they read? Is it blogs, books, magazines, journals etc.?
- What TV shows or YouTube channels do they watch?
- Which experts do they listen to?
- Are there certain websites they follow?
- Who are the big names in their industry that they look up to?
- What sort of conferences or events are they most likely to attend?
- Which podcasts or radio shows do they listen to?
- Are they going to be on Facebook or another social media platform?
- Social media preferences – are they listeners, watchers or readers?
- What are their main pain points?
- Do they have any specific buying habits?
- Which clubs and associations would they be most likely to attend?
- What are the goals, values, aspirations and dreams of your target audience?

Summary

It's important to understand that even if you've done your research on a very deep level, your marketing will actually be informed by a mixture of understanding your market (the research part) and making educated guesses.

- Basic demographics include age, gender, where they live, income level, marital status, whether or not they are a homeowner, education level.
- **GOLDEN RULE – be specific and not general with your demographics** because 80% of your target market will likely fall under the same demographics.
- You can learn a ton about your ideal market through a variety of techniques, including surveying your list and doing Google searches on the best or top blogs, websites, forums etc.
- If you have no idea where to start or you're just starting out, then researching your competitors and reverse engineering your products and services are the best places to start.

In Part 2 of this book, we'll look at how you can start building out your products and services – starting with shifting the way you feel about selling.

Part 2: Building Out Your Products and Services

One of the biggest reasons why offers fail comes down to an inability to really dig deep into the needs of your ideal audience. I've seen it time and again: experts creating products and services they THINK their audience want and will pay for – but when it comes to selling, they're unable to make them work.

Not you, however.

By now, you should have really started putting the process of Mind-Hack™ Marketing into practice. You now know who your avatar is, and you've identified the unmet needs your ideal prospect has – and this alone will put you ahead of the curve. When you start building out your products and services, you'll be doing it with real insight, and not on an idea or a whim of what you think might or might not work.

But building out your products and services is only part of the equation. Having the right mindset to charge high fees and sell effectively is another thing entirely. Get this wrong, and all your hard work will never pay off because you'll never have the confidence to sell with authenticity.

That's why we'll kick the following chapter off with the mindset of selling. Once you've understood this, we'll look at value-based selling and the premise of testing your ideas before taking them to market.

These elements alone will ensure you've got the firm foundations for marketing and selling offers your ideal audience want, need and will pay for.

Let's get started!

Chapter 6:
The Mindset of Selling

I'm a firm believer that selling should be an easy and pleasurable experience for your audience. If you've implemented everything in the previous chapters, you've done the hard work of getting the right people into your world and getting them excited about how you can help them overcome their challenges and problems through your offers.

However, when it comes to selling, this is where many businesses struggle. I've seen everything, from the "hammer them with offers until they buy" approach to "people will come to the conclusion on their own" approach, and everything in between.

The only thing that matters to your prospect is this:

They LOVE to buy, but HATE being sold to.

Think about it – you want to buy on YOUR terms and not because someone is trying to push you into a sale.

It's essential you understand the difference between buying and selling and the mindset that goes behind the buying process. That's why in this chapter, we're going to delve into the mindset of selling. Specifically, I'll go into the buying cycle as well as talking about the value you create for your audience.

The Myths and Misconceptions About Selling

One of the biggest myths in selling is that you can "sell to everyone". Hopefully, you should have figured out by now that this isn't the case – in fact, far from it!

Unless you're selling a commodity, you really shouldn't be selling to everyone! Instead, you should be selling to a select segment of the market. Even better, you should be ultra-specific about who your avatars are (most businesses will have more than one) and sell to each of them accordingly. I'll show you exactly how to do this later in this book.

A huge myth about selling is that customers only care about price – a false assumption at best. Unless you're selling a commodity, pricing is rarely an issue. As you've already seen in previous chapters, there are many reasons why people buy or don't buy, and money is rarely one of them!

Instead, customers care about the value they receive in exchange for their money. If they see the value of what you're selling, they have a need AND they resonate with you, they'll buy.

This brings me nicely onto another huge myth – and that's the myth about competitive selling. Your competition may well have a better product or offer, but the truth is prospects only buy from those they know, like and trust AND with whom they have built a personal connection.

Your competitor can't copy the relationship you have with

your audience – period. Empathy will go a LONG way in helping to secure a sale. If you've done your job properly, your audience will make an EMPOWERED buying decision.

An empowered buying decision is when your audience has all the information they need to make a buying decision AND they feel comfortable buying at their own pace and need – and not because you practically pushed them into a sale.

Believe it or not, when customers request a refund, many times it will be because the said customer only bought from you to get you off their back. One of the biggest "weapons" that sales reps use is forcing prospects to spend time with them, because it's been proven that the greater your exposure to a brand, the more likely you are to buy from them.

This is one of the reasons why time-share companies will invite you to an all-day open event which is nothing more than a glorified sales pitch. In fact, time-share companies in particular have horrible reputations as being THE snakes of the industry because they practically force you into buying time-shares from them.

I remember very clearly being in the unfortunate position of having a salesman in my home who was trying to sell me into a contract for a payment machine.

No matter what I did, I just couldn't get rid of him. In the end, I signed up after listening to him drone on and on for two hours. I wasn't happy with the sale and immediately tried to cancel thereafter – a process they made painfully difficult, and which took several months.

After months of trying to cancel my agreement (and being charged in the process), I felt I had no choice but to vent on social media. It wasn't until I left a nasty comment on their Facebook page that they FINALLY backed off.

We live in the age of social media and online reviews, where anyone can say anything about you – so be careful about how you treat your prospects.

Another big myth about selling is that sales is a numbers game. Well, technically, this one is both a myth and a hard truth. Yes, you MUST know your numbers and have targets to aspire to.

That being said, how you think about your prospects is going to make a huge difference to your bottom line. When you ONLY focus on sales as numbers on a spreadsheet, it becomes easy to remove the emotion from the sale and resort to the hard sell.

Your audience isn't stupid. They can smell pushy and sleazy sales tactics from a mile off. That's why it's hyper-critical to focus on helping prospects make an empowered buying decision based on real want and need and not because you've got revenue goals to achieve.

This value-based sales approach is a far superior way of turning prospects into paying customers. Let's examine this further.

Value-Based Selling

Value-based selling focuses on aligning your products and services with what your prospects want, need and will pay for. In other words, it's ALL about the prospect and NEVER about YOU.

Value-based selling is a far superior way to sell than being pushy or salesy, because it's all about helping prospects find a solution to their unmet needs. These can be either problems or desires.

Either way, the golden rule of selling is this: **sell people what they want, but give them what they need.**

While it might sound like a cliché, it is in fact true. People buy on emotional needs or wants, and then justify their purchase with logic. By finding out what a prospect REALLY wants early on in the sales process, selling becomes much easier.

For example, a person might need to lose weight, but what they actually want is to feel confident in their own skin and look great in skinny jeans. See the difference?

To help you, there are five specific principles of value-based selling which are as follows:

1) Know your customer – This one should be kind of obvious by now! Knowing exactly what your prospect wants, needs, desires, fears and is frustrated by will go a LONG way in helping you secure the sale. Asking key questions around their goals, desires and unmet needs will give you the insights you need in order to help your prospects make an empowered buying decision.

2) Share the value – Don't automatically assume your prospect knows the value your product or service provides. You've got to clearly communicate how your product or service is going to solve their problem and change or improve your prospect's life.

3) Educate first – I'll reiterate what I said earlier: people are not stupid. In fact, consumers today are pretty sophisticated and like to feel smart and informed. Wherever possible, educate your prospect on why your product or service is superior. The easiest way to do this is by asking prospects what their challenges are and then giving them clarity on their situation.

4) Don't rush the prospect – While a sales call shouldn't drag on for hours, you don't want to rush the prospect into a buying decision. Painting the picture of what life looks like when they've solved their issue will keep the conversation on track and help the prospect come to the natural conclusion that they want what you have to offer.

5) Figure out what prospects value most – People pay for speed and ease. If there's a faster, easier way to do something, there's always going to be a willing crowd to buy. People also pay for things like saving money, saving time, feeling more

secure, etc. You need to figure out what people value the most and remind them of it in your pitch.

The ideal solution for any prospect is buying something because they believe it to be good for them, and also that it's THEIR idea – not yours. This is KEY in value-based selling.

You'll find the selling process is much easier when you explore the emotions with your prospects and dig deep into why they want what you have to offer.

In my two-day Mind-Hack™ Marketing workshop, I look in detail at how to do this for yourself and really dig deep into your ideal customer. To learn more, simply go to: http://arfasairaiqbal.com/mindhackresources.

MVPs and Testing

I'm a huge fan of taking a customer-centric approach to creating offers. Most businesses create products first and then take them to market in the hope they can sell them to a hungry crowd – without even verifying if the market wants these products or not.

It's a top-down approach at best and highly inefficient. Case in point, there are millions of ideas, products and programmes out there that never saw the light of day. How many business owners have tried and failed to make an idea or an offer work?

Probably too many to count! Course creators are just one

example of this phenomenon. The number of coaches, consultants and other experts who've created programmes and courses they struggle to sell likely runs into the millions.

That's where an MVP or "minimum viable product" can really help. An MVP is when you test an idea with your market without building or creating all of it first. It's a fantastic way to see if your market is interested enough in your idea to want to pay for it, and collect feedback in the process.

Not only that, but an MVP can go a long way in helping you to mitigate risk in your business. Just imagine spending tens of thousands trying to launch an idea that falls flat on its face!

For larger businesses, it's not a massive problem. However, for a smaller business, it can literally bring the business to its knees. One of my previous clients spent two years developing a programme which cost him well over six figures to create and launch – and despite throwing EVERYTHING (and I do mean everything) at trying to make his offer work, he couldn't get it to sell.

Worse, my client wound up in SERIOUS debt and almost lost his house because of it. On the contrary, I've worked with clients who've launched with an IDEA and it's taken off like a rocket. My preference is always to test an idea and create an MVP FIRST, before you go to market.

If you've understood your avatar correctly and have done a deep dive into your ideal customer, you should know exactly what they want and need. By starting with your ideal customer in mind, you're less likely to create an offer that fails and more likely to produce a winning idea.

Moreover, pushing a winning idea means you have proof of concept from your audience BEFORE you go into full-on build mode. In my own business, I've sold services that don't even exist – except in my head.

I remember a few years back I'd had a particularly quiet month and needed at least £2,500 to pay my rent and bills. I got to work crafting an offer which I emailed out to my TINY list of just 85 people at the time. By the third email, I'd sold a "Rapid Funnel Get It Done Day" for £2,500 – and the money was in my account three days before rent was due!

When done properly, you can virtually create demand out of thin air – or so it seems! The brilliant thing about MVPs is that they are pretty lean to implement compared to a full-scale offer and are strategically designed to test proof of concept as well as collect feedback so you can improve the MVP.

However, an MVP is rarely about making profit (bonus points if you do!) but it IS about understanding market demand and ensuring it's fit for purpose. Most businesses that use MVPs will be more interested in solving problems, gathering data and figuring out pricing and positioning.

There are plenty of ways you can introduce MVPs into your business, depending on what you do. Here are a few to get you going:

- Launching a course, programme or software as a "beta" version.
- Pre-selling an idea for a programme/product.
- Getting people onto a waiting list for a product/programme launch.
- Creating a limited stock/limited capacity version of an offer.
- Inviting users to become testers for products.
- Offering trial sizes or free trials of products (think subscription boxes or software subscriptions).
- Creating prototypes and selling on pre-order only – crowdfunding campaigns are a classic example of this in action.

Action Points

Here are some action points you can implement in your own business to see if an offer would actually work:

- Ask your audience! A survey, quiz or feedback loop of some kind is invaluable in trying to figure out what the market wants.
- Check comments on social media – you'd be surprised at how much GOLD is buried in comments in forums, groups, blog posts and other social media platforms where

---

your ideal clients hang out. Look out for the following:
- What are people complaining about?
- What are they asking for?
- Where are they getting stuck?
- Is it a common issue that no one has found a solution to yet?
- Analyse your competitors and figure out the pros and cons of their offers. What's missing that people want?
- Once you've formulated an idea, ASK your audience if they would be interested in it – a poll inside a Facebook group, for example, could work really well.

As you can see, there's no need to launch any product into a market blind. Savvy businesses will instead launch an MVP and save themselves a lot of time and hassle in the process.

One of my clients (a multi-eight-figure therapy training provider) launched a 16-week programme for their therapists as a beta programme. This was a brand-new programme they were looking at launching to the mass market – but they needed proof of concept.

I wrote a sales letter to get a test group of 30 therapists on board for free in exchange for their participation in the programme and in-depth feedback and video testimonials.

The beta group diligently went through the programme and my client got a ton of useful feedback, which they used to improve the programme before launching to the market. Plus, they also had lots of incredible testimonials to boot!

Coming Full Circle

Hopefully at this point in the book, you're in a good place with understanding your ideal customers and also now understanding how this information fits with the mindset of selling. The two are intertwined. Selling is based on psychology and knowing who your customer is.

The greater your knowledge about your ideal customer, the easier it becomes to sell – especially when you meet prospects where they are at and take a value-based approach to selling.

Self-Worth

How does self-worth determine success? How do thoughts, feelings and emotions affect how you charge clients? In this section, we'll find out by taking a look at pricing and positioning and why commoditising yourself is always a bad idea.

Charging the Fees You Deserve

It took a LONG time for me to feel comfortable with the rates

I'm charging today. If you're a service provider in particular, then charging the fees you deserve can be a touchy or difficult subject.

I've met people who exude confidence and, therefore, even with their lack of experience, charge hefty fees. I've also met people with years of experience who are brilliant at what they do, but they have never broken away from trading time for money.

Charging per hour is a horrible model to follow because it's impossible to scale your time, which means you're constantly at the mercy of the number of hours you work.

More often than not, many experts have a secret fear around charging high fees. For example, a coach might think it sounds extortionate to say "I charge £200/hr", so they settle on rates that are a fraction of what they could be.

The reasons why you might undercharge are numerous but include:

- Not seeing the value of what you do and therefore aligning your rates with the rates of manual labour costs.
- Fear of being unable to get results for clients.
- Feeling like a fraud (also known as imposter syndrome).
- Insecurity or lack of confidence in your skills.
- Worried you'll be seen as taking advantage of clients.
- Getting the wrong clients on board who don't value what you do.
- Anxiety due to a previous bad experience.

- You're not thinking like a business owner.

Regardless of why you undercharge, the most important thing to remember is that if you don't build profit into your business model, you'll never make any. It's also highly unethical to charge per hour. The reason why I believe charging per hour is unethical is because a client has no idea how many "sessions" they need to get the desired outcome.

Back in January 2021, I had a back injury that resulted in two herniated discs in my lower back, and I was told by my doctor that I needed surgery. Keen to avoid the knife, I found myself a chiropractor who happened to charge per hour.

Hunched over and limping into the chiro's office, I was given a quick 20-minute consultation plus an adjustment. The chiro said I'd need weekly chiropractic treatments to recover, so I started going every week. Every time I asked the chiro how long it would take to start feeling better, she would say things like, "Let's aim to get you better in a few weeks."

Every time I went to the clinic, I felt like I was being rushed and not really taken good care of. After six weeks and zero improvement, I decided to stop my sessions because I was still hunched over, still limping and still popping painkillers like sweets every four hours. It was really frustrating!

Determined not to have surgery, I didn't give up. I found an alternative clinic that's pretty far from where I live. Based on the outstanding reviews, I thought I should at least give it a go – and nervously booked myself in. Wow, the difference between the two clinics was amazing!

My initial consultation lasted an entire hour, during which my chiro went through my MRI results and really took her time to go through my medical history. She tested my strength, my walk, reflexes and asked me a ton of questions.

After the consultation, I was asked to return the next day to discuss my results. Again, my chiro really took her time and explained everything to me in detail, including why my body was in so much pain, how long it would take for me to recover and what to expect in terms of treatment.

I was given a 12–18-month timeframe to get better, and my treatment plan included traction therapy and massage too. I was given a full treatment breakdown and a package price – it was eye-wateringly expensive, but I happily paid it in full because my chiro gave me something the other clinic couldn't: confidence that they could actually help me.

At the end of the day, clients only care about results. That's it. As you should have learned by now, when people don't buy, it's very rarely about the money.

While the first clinic charged a low fee per session, they gave me zero confidence I would even get better! Looking back, of course they were rushing me in every appointment – because how on earth could they afford to run the clinic unless they packed it with clients!

The second clinic, on the other hand, managed my

ations really well and gave me a full treatment plan. Yes, I paid a lot of money – but I left with the certainty that they could help me, and they didn't disappoint!

Your clients and customers are no different. It's important to understand that first and foremost your audience only cares about the results/outcome/transformation/benefits you provide – anything else is secondary.

Also, clients are usually in the dark on how long something takes, because they often don't understand how something works or what it involves. For example, take two experts who do web design and both charge an hourly rate. Expert A is highly inexperienced. Expert B is brilliant at what they do but struggles with low confidence.

Expert A charges £20/hr and takes 20 hours to produce a website, which comes to a total of £400. Expert B, on the other hand, charges the same rate but does a much better job. However, because they are highly experienced, they only take half as long as Expert A to do the job, but sadly only get paid half the amount.

Does this sound fair to you? Clearly not!

Furthermore, the client for Expert A might think they're getting a bargain for just £20/hr but gets a shock when they're handed the final invoice, because they assumed the work would only take 8–10 hours.

See the problem? To make matters worse, BOTH experts

need a LOT of clients at £20/hr just to make enough money to live on – there really isn't any room for fun or even having a decent lifestyle. To make any meaningful amount of income, both experts are most likely to be overworked and stressed out trying to find clients.

To add insult to injury, at those rates, there's no room in the budget to spend on marketing, and this means both experts will almost certainly experience boom-and-bust cycles in their business.

Hopefully, you're beginning to get the picture as to why charging per hour is actually a horrible and unethical pricing model. When I work with experts who offer services, I usually take them through my Scaling Calculator™ which clearly shows them the optimum pricing they need to charge in order to create time and financial freedom for themselves.

How Should You Price Your Offers?

If charging per hour is out, then how should you be charging? In this section, I want to help you figure out your pricing and, more importantly, how you need to restructure your offer to create flexibility and freedom in your business.

Two things to take into account are your yearly and monthly goals and the number of clients you can serve easily. Once you know what this looks like, you need to figure out how many of each product or service you need to sell per year to hit your profit goal.

Let's walk through an example:

1. **How much do you want to earn per month?**
   £20,000

2. **How many hours do you want to work per week?**
   20 hours a week or 80 hours a month.

3. **How much do you want to work per year, factoring in holidays?**
   Two months of holiday a year means you're working 10 months (or 800 hours).

4. **What's your revenue goal per year?**
   £200,000 (working 10 months).

5. **Work out the total value per hour of your time.**
   £200,000 (a year)/10 (months)/80 (hours a month) = £250/hr

In this example, if a coach wants to make £20,000 per month, they're looking at an hourly rate of £250 – a far cry from the "usual" hourly rates I hear of anywhere between £20 and £50!

This means in any one week for you to hit your monthly revenue goal, you need to be earning a minimum of £5,000 a WEEK or £1,000 a DAY (assuming you don't work weekends).

Even on an hourly rate of £100, you'd need to be working at LEAST 10 hours a day to hit those numbers, or 50 hours a week. No matter how passionate you are about what you do, I don't think being stressed out, burnt out and exhausted is what anyone wants.

This is why charging per hour just doesn't work for experts and service providers. Instead, you need to be thinking about packages, programmes and incentives based on the value you provide.

I've listed below the "typical" ranges of pricing structures that work for coaches, consultants and other experts:

- Virtual Private Intensive (VIP Day): £700 to £3,000
- In-Person Private Intensive (VIP Day): £1,500 to £20,000
- Masterminds: £1,200 to £100,000
- Live Events: £297 to £4,500
- Virtual Events: £97 to £497
- Information Products: £7 to £5,000
- Continuity/Membership/Association: £27 to £497/month
- Three-Month Private Programme: £1,500 to £10,000
- Six-Month Private Programme: £3,000 to £15,000
- 12-Month Private Programme: £10,000 to £100,000
- 12-Month Group Programme: £5,000 to £50,000
- Certification and Licensing: £2,000 to £20,000 (+ monthly or yearly licence fees)
- Virtual Training (Bootcamps, Teleseminars, Webinars): £97 to £1,997
- Group Coaching Programmes: Usually ⅓ of the price of a regular programme.

You may well be looking at these prices and feeling a little overwhelmed as to how you can implement these in your business, or you may be wondering how you can possibly charge high fees for your programmes – and that's what this next section is all about!

Commodity vs High-Ticket

The "expert" space is rapidly growing. It seems as if everyone is either a coach, consultant or other expert.

The average yearly income of a coach, for example, is around £32,561 in the UK[9] and between $47,000 in the USA[10]. By the time you've paid for business and personal expenses, there isn't much cash left in the bank for you to enjoy yourself.

In fact, most experts (as already mentioned above) are overworked and underpaid due to charging hourly rates. So what's the difference between an expert who is struggling and an expert who is living the freedom lifestyle?

The difference comes down to being a specialist versus a generalist, because a generalist is actually similar to a commodity. A commodity by its very nature is subject to market value and, sadly, vastly restrained by it.

In terms of physical products, a packet of crisps is a great example of a commodity. There's a surplus of demand and

---

[9] Reed UK, (2021), 'Average Salary Checker', available at: https://www.reed.co.uk/average-salary/average-coach-salary
[10] Zippia, (2021), 'Average Coach Salary', available at: https://www.zippia.com/coach-jobs/salary/

a ton of choice. No matter how hard you try, you can never charge more than the market value of another packet of crisps. Their value or monetary worth can never exceed what the market is willing to pay for it because it can EASILY be replaced by another brand.

Experts are no different. The expert industry has been growing year on year for several years now, with no signs of slowing down. This means there are more and more experts entering the marketplace every single day.

However, the difference between a high-paid expert and one who is barely scraping by really does have a lot to do with how specialised they are.

A doctor who is a general practitioner can never charge more than the market rate because they are a generalist. A heart surgeon, on the other hand, can make many times that of a general practitioner because they specialise in one field.

Let me illustrate with a coach as an example. Coach A is a generalist and sells "coaching sessions" at £30 a session. Coach B is a specialist confidence coach – so who can charge more?

Coach B of course! But, as you'll see in the next chapter, whilst being a specialist will definitely help you increase your fees, it's not enough to command premium rates.

Premium rates are actually as a careful result of your offers as the ONLY choice your prospects talk more about premium positioning in the next chapter.

Summary

In this chapter, we talked about the mindset of selling, and specifically, we covered the following:

- Testing your offers is key before taking them to market – not only does it save you time and money, it helps you understand if the market actually wants what you have.
- Charging per hour is a horrible business model because it doesn't allow you to grow and keeps you stuck in cycles of boom and bust.
- A value-based selling approach is a much more powerful and profitable way to sustainably grow and scale your business.

In the next chapter, we take a look at one of the most important factors in helping you to charge your worth and get it – and that's how you position yourself.

Chapter 7: Positioning

In the previous chapter, I talked about why it's unethical to charge hourly rates and why specialising will help you charge higher prices. I also shared with you a formula for figuring out your ideal hourly rate, as well as what kind of pricing you could be charging for your offers.

In this chapter, I want to take things further by sharing some of the inside secrets elite experts use to get to, and stay at, the top of their game – and it's simpler than it seems. A fair warning though: while it sounds simple, it requires hard work, discipline and consistent work. That being said, if you've applied everything I've talked about so far in *Mind-Hack™ Marketing*, you should already have a distinct advantage over your competitors.

High Fees vs Package Prices – What's the Difference?

The difference between a heart surgeon who commands seven figures a year and one who is doing multiple six figures is actually in their unique process/system/method or technique. This is known as a "signature system or method" and is your proprietary process of how you achieve a particular outcome.

For example, imagine you have two coaches who are both specialists in their field: Coach Anna and Coach Mia. Anna is a confidence coach who offers a three-month package of coaching sessions to help you feel more confident and charges £1,200 for 12 coaching sessions.

Anna keeps an open niche and works with women and makes a healthy income – but nowhere near enough to enjoy true financial freedom.

Mia is also a confidence coach, but she has a different approach. She doesn't sell a "package" of sessions. Instead, she has a three-step system called "Endless Confidence" which is designed to take women entrepreneurs from shy to super confident in just 12 weeks. While any coach in the world can teach women confidence, only Mia can teach "Endless Confidence" – the exclusivity of the system alone makes her immediately more valuable, and in demand, compared to Anna.

As a result, Mia works part time and gets to spend lots of time with her family while making multi-six figures with ease. She loves her work, and clients seek her out, paying £5,000 at minimum just to work with her. This is the beauty of having a signature system or process. It's your proprietary process of how to achieve the result your clients are looking for.

Here's how you benefit from having a signature system in place:

- Instantly makes your experience compelling and more marketable.
- Positions you as a highly sought-after "go-to" person in your industry.
- Differentiates you from your competitors.

- Boosts your credibility and expertise so you can command high fees.
- The client attraction process becomes easier and smoother.
- The repeatable process makes clients' results predictable and consistent.
- Removes the guesswork from knowing what to do with your prospects.
- Reduces overwhelm when creating your content, because your content is based on your system.
- You can splinter or break off parts of your system and sell them as a stand-alone solution for clients.
- Your signature system can become the basis of a book, further lending you credibility and giving you authority in your field as a top expert.
- Allows you to scale easily as you can sell courses, group programmes, private programmes and masterminds, and you can even teach other experts your signature system as licensees.

The beauty of a signature system is you can grow as much as you want to – by introducing the right people and systems in your business, you can become the "Tony Robbins" of your own industry!

And all of this starts with figuring out what your proprietary process looks like. There are nine steps to defining your signature solution. The following questions will help you do this properly:

1. What result or outcome will your client receive?

...ite down everything you do to help your clients get results in a sequential way, from start to finish.

3. Distil these steps into a three-, five-, seven- or nine-step process.
4. For each of these steps, identify all the sub-steps in sequential order.
5. What's the result or outcome of each main step?
6. For every step in your process, what implementation tools do you need/use or develop?
7. Name every step in your process.
8. Give your entire system a cool name.
9. Last but not least, go ahead and trademark your shiny new signature system!

The Problem Ladder

Once you have your signature system, it makes it easier to figure out what your clients need on their journey. This is critical because every time you solve a problem for your client, it usually opens up a brand-new problem for them.

Knowing and understanding what this looks like for your ideal client is essential to creating the perfect customer journey. Let's walk through an example.

Imagine a coach who has just started out and is now looking to get clients. Their first problem is trying to find qualified leads. They want a regular income and need positive cash flow on a month-to-month basis.

Once they've solved this problem, their next problem might

be a conversion issue. They're getting good quality leads but don't have a proper system in place to turn more of those leads into actual consultation or strategy calls.

Further down the line when they've solved the conversion problem, their next problem might be that they're not closing as many prospects into paying clients.

Another problem might be that the coach feels trapped in the dollars-per-hour model and wants to transition from selling their time to selling based on value – in other words, they are looking to sell high-ticket.

Once they've solved the high-ticket problem, they may now be in a position to grow their business – so now they have a brand-new problem, which is they are looking to scale but don't know how.

Finally, once they've solved their scaling problem, it may be that the coach now wants to become a thought leader and rapidly grow their revenue – of course, this presents another problem. And so on and so forth.

The key thing to remember is that each problem your ideal client faces presents a new opportunity to sell or upsell them a solution based on your signature system. You may even have other programmes that don't fit into your signature system which are a good "next fit" for potential clients.

The point is there's ALWAYS somewhere for them to go. When the client can no longer grow with you, they'll move on to find someone who CAN help them.

The cool thing about this scenario is that when you know your ideal client really well, you'll know what their problems are and you should have solutions ready to help them. Even better, any prospect at any stage can come to you and, based on what they need, you can prescribe them a solution bespoke to them.

Prospects don't just enter your world right at the beginning of their journey – they can join you at any stage of growth. The point is there's always somewhere for them to go – and this is why knowing the sequence of problems (sometimes problems are not sequential) your ideal client is likely to experience is going to be to your advantage.

Each client has a different need depending on where they are in their journey, and for each need, I have a solution that's viable for them. For example, I've worked with coaches and consultants who are starting out and wanting to differentiate themselves from other experts, right through to multi-eight-figure celebrity/influencer coaches, consultants and therapists who are looking to push and promote their programmes to a larger audience.

Problem Ladder Exercise
Here's a simple exercise for you to try.

I actually put this information into a spreadsheet so it's easy to refer to, but also easy for my salesperson to understand what to offer to potential clients based on where they are stuck:

1. List at least three big/main problems your ideal client faces that you could potentially help with. These problems may or may not be in sequential order.
2. What does your ideal client want?
3. What do they actually need?
4. For each problem, which part of your system could help them? This could be an entire step from your signature system, or it could even be a sub-step from your system.
5. What's the investment for your ideal client to solve each of these problems?

Need more help? I have a "Signature Program Intensive" to help my clients redesign their offers and turn them into highly compelling programmes so they can command premium fees.

Not only does the intensive program include an in-depth deep dive into the problem ladder, but I also show you how much your time is worth and how to price and structure your programmes, as well as how to talk about your signature solution so you can attract more of your ideal clients.

If that's something you need help with and would like to find out more, simply go to: http://arfasairaiqbal.com/mindhackresources.

Summary

In Part 2, we talked about building out your products and programmes and, specifically, I covered the mindset of selling and how you can charge your worth and get it.

Here are some of the key concepts we talked about:

- Charging your worth is based on a combination of creating your signature solution and having the right mindset.
- Value-based selling outperforms traditional selling techniques which often rely on high-pressure tactics.
- Products and programmes should never be developed without first testing the concept with your market. If you can't sell the idea, you'll struggle to sell the programme.
- Trading time for money is a horrible model to follow and keeps you stuck, struggling and exhausted. It's also unethical, in my view!

In Part 3, we'll be looking at the nuances of building out your campaigns and how to start implementing everything you've learned so far.

Part 3: Building Out Your Campaigns

In the final part of this book, we'll be doing a deep dive into the nuances of building out your campaigns. We're taking all the information we've covered so far and translating it into a working and actionable plan for your business – everything from this point onwards is about to get really exciting! This is literally Mind-Hack™ Marketing in action!

Specifically, we'll look at the different stages of a funnel and how to plan and execute every stage so you can confidently crush your income goals. Everything in this section is about high profitability and ensuring you have the greatest chance of success with your campaigns.

I'll share some of the secret ninja tips and tricks I've discovered from working in this space as a direct response copywriter for well over a decade and getting some pretty awesome results too!

A word of warning though: regardless of the best planning in the world, be prepared to split test EVERYTHING. Everything you've discovered so far in this book will massively help you produce the best campaigns possible with the highest chance of converting.

However, as every top marketing expert on the planet will tell you, sometimes things (for multiple reasons) just don't work out that way. This is why split testing is essential to the success of your campaigns, and I'll be covering this later in this book.

In the next chapter, we'll be covering the Perpetual Profit System™ – a seamless way to create profitable marketing campaigns from all the hard work you've done so far.

Chapter 8: The Perpetual Profit System™

Introduction to the Perpetual Profit System™

This is where the fun begins! It's what I like to call the execution path, where all of the work you've done in the previous chapters comes together in a full-blown campaign.

Specifically, I'm going to show you how to create your lead magnets, tripwires and sales funnels by reverse engineering your products. I'm also going to show you how to go super deep with your ad targeting.

Making money from your ads does require a lot of thought – and there are lots of things you need to take into consideration to ensure your ads are profitable, from the amount you spend to the revenue you bring in, to the platforms you decide to use. You should be able to track everything AND you should be able to understand HOW to scale ads correctly and measure input and output.

So everything I'm going to share with you in this chapter is going to help you create powerful campaigns that convert. You've done the groundwork and not only do you understand who your ideal customer is, but you know where to find them and, more importantly, you understand why they may or may not buy from you.

Your next step involves turning all of your knowledge into

actionable campaigns so you can start benefiting from more sales and more profit!

Every concept in this chapter is strategic, incredibly powerful and applicable to almost every industry. It doesn't matter if you're a doctor looking to grow a practice or a corporate entity looking to wow customers and clients. In fact, the concepts in this chapter are evergreen. In other words, they'll be relevant even 100 years from now, so you'll never struggle for a marketing campaign ever again.

Regardless of how many products you create, you can simply rinse and repeat the process. In this chapter, I'll give you seven key questions your marketing MUST cover at the very minimum. I call this my "Mirror Matrix" because you'll essentially mirror the questions you ask about your customers for your own brand.

Any content you create about your brand, your company, your offer etc., must answer those seven key questions, and this exercise alone is enough for you to see a huge improvement in your metrics.

Some of the exercises in this chapter are quite intensive and require a LOT of thinking, but I promise you, they are well worth your time to go through.

For now, let's discuss the three ways you can grow a business, since these principles will underpin everything we do going forward.

We've already touched on this in previous chapters, but it's so important that it's worth revisiting. Marketing legend Jay Abraham[11] says there are only three ways to grow a business:

- Increasing the number of customers.
- Increasing the Average Order Frequency (AOF).
- Increasing the Average Order Value (AOV).

Whatever challenges you have with growing your business, I can guarantee they will almost always fall into one of these three categories...

The cost involved in acquiring new customers is not only one of the biggest costs you'll ever have in your business, it's also one of the MAJOR reasons why businesses go bust.

This is because increasing your customer base means you must spend more to acquire them... and this can create massive cash flow problems which can land you in a LOT of trouble.

However, there is a MUCH deeper principle at work that underpins the growth of your business, one which I believe supersedes the three principles of growth as mentioned by Jay Abraham, and that's this: **Knowing your ideal customers (or avatar) better than they know themselves!**

There is a direct positive correlation between businesses that know and understand their ideal customers really well

---

[11] Jay Abraham, 'Three Ways to Grow Your Business', Abraham Group, available at: https://www.abraham.com/topic/three-ways-to-grow-your-business/

and the amount of money they make.

For most business owners, their primary focus is naturally on selling more of their products and services. This usually means increasing the number of customers, selling them more goods and getting them to come back more often.

Going back to what Jay Abraham says, let's explore this in more detail...

Increasing the Number of Customers

Of all the activities a business will engage in, ***acquiring customers has the greatest cost attached to it***. The process of getting a paying customer starts with finding the right prospects, getting them to become a lead, and then eventually converting leads into paying customers.

In essence, this is what a sales funnel is. Your job as a business owner is to create awareness of your products and services and then turn that awareness into leads and sales.

It can be a long and sometimes complicated process and involves a mix of content, paid, referral, social media and email marketing. As I said before, the most amount of money is spent in acquiring a customer...

However, this creates a problem: unfortunately, there's the assumption that doubling the traffic to your website will automatically double your sales – and that's not true!

This is flawed thinking and can mean thousands of pounds in wasted ad spend.

Every lead source has a tipping point – the point where spending more will result in diminishing returns due to factors such as:

- Ad management costs
- Lower search volume
- The changing behaviour of your audience.

It's the reason why ad management agencies have to constantly find and test new audiences and change-up ads to avoid "ad fatigue".

And because increasing customers is where the most amount of effort, energy and money is spent, it's therefore absolutely CRITICAL you market to the right people ALL the time. We'll get to this in a moment.

Increasing the Average Order Frequency (AOF)

The average order frequency (AOF) simply means the number of times your customers bought from you in any given period.

Getting customers to repeatedly buy from you requires a mixture of having the right offerings that are of value to your ideal customer and then staying in front of them through various means of marketing.

Increasing the Average Order Value (AOV)

The average order value (AOV) is simply the average total of every order a customer places with you over a defined period of time. AOV is an important metric for online businesses because it drives key decisions such as advertising spend and product pricing.

Here's the thing – in order for any business to scale and grow to its fullest potential, you need to increase the number of ideal customers you have, the AOV and the AOF.

But, there's a fundamental truth in truly being able to make the kind of money you've always dreamed of, which very few people actually talk about, and that's this:

ALL three of these factors are FULLY DEPENDENT on how well you understand your customers. PERIOD.

Powerful and effective marketing can only happen when a business understands the audience they are serving – and more importantly, understands the challenges, pain points, desires, fears and frustrations of their target market.

You can have an enormous list with extremely low engagement, meaning you'll make very little money. You can equally have a tiny list that is hyper-responsive and buys everything you sell them – and all because you took the time to understand your ideal customers.

By now, you already know that ALL of your content, social

media posts, lead magnets, tripwires, ad campaigns, sales funnels and everything in between should be 100% guided by the needs of your ideal customer.

Key business decisions, such as offering new products and services and creating new marketing campaigns, should NEVER be discussed in isolation without going back to your ideal customer and figuring out what they need BEFORE you start creating new offerings!

The businesses that understand their ideal customers (in detail) are the businesses that make the most amount of money AND create lifelong loyalty with their audience.

This is exactly why we've covered so much of this in detail early on in previous chapters.

In fact, understanding your ideal customer is the difference between businesses that make six figures and businesses that make seven or more figures a year.

As we progress, you'll see exactly how your campaigns will start coming to life by taking these core principles and superimposing the psychology of your avatar over them.

For now, let's figure out how aware your avatar is of your offers.

How Aware Is Your Market?

Back in 1966, copywriting legend Eugene Schwartz wrote an

incredible book called *Breakthrough Advertising*[12]. In it, he shared many fantastic insights – insights that allowed him to sell over ONE BILLION (yes, that's not a mistake!) dollars' worth of products in his lifetime.

I managed to get hold of his book a while back, and while the entire book is full of gold, one thing in particular really stood out for me – and that's the **Market Awareness Model**.

The Market Awareness Model is so incredibly simple, yet the ingenuity of why it's so powerful does indeed lie in its simplicity. Eugene mentioned five levels of awareness that prospects have in relation to your products and services – and how you communicate with your market is very much determined by the stage at which your prospect is.

These five stages move from "unaware" – "problem aware" – "solution aware" – "product aware" – and finally "most aware" (or hyper-aware) of you and your solutions. The more aware someone is of you, the less work is needed to move that person from a prospect to a buyer.

So what does each stage actually mean and how is this relevant to the way in which you communicate with your market? To help answer this, I found this diagram online that neatly summarises the key points of what you need to know:

---

[12] Eugene M. Schwartz, (2017), Breakthrough Advertising, Titans Marketing

What Kind of Copy Should We Write?
Eugene Schwartz's "Five Levels of Awareness"

Most Aware	Product Aware	Solution Aware	Problem Aware	Unaware
←				→
Direct				Indirect
Product and Price	Discounts and Deals	Claims and Proof	Benefits and Anxieties	Stories and Secrets

Source: Great Leads by Michael Masterson and John Forde

1. **The Unaware Stage** – The majority of your market. This group of people are completely unaware of the problem your product solves. In fact, they have no idea you exist, which means that even though they are your target market, they have no idea who you are and what you can do for them. To move someone from being "unaware" to "most aware" requires a LOT of education and hard work. Pull people in with stories, case studies and excellent content that speaks to general issues the potential prospects are facing.

2. **Problem Aware Stage** – People who fall into this segment of your market are aware they have a problem and they know they need to have it fixed. However, at this stage, they have no idea that you are the solution for them. This is where you amp up your marketing and take it up a notch – videos and webinars would work really well at this stage.

3. **Solution Aware Stage** – These people know there are

several solutions for their problem, but they don't know about your product or service. This group of people are actively looking to have their problem solved and so, to ensure they make the right decision, you need to hit them with facts and figures and case studies etc. to move them to the next stage.

4. **Product Aware Stage** – At this stage in the game, prospects know you and your competitors and are making a decision about what to do and who to go with. Hit them with deals, discounts, free trials and demonstrations of HOW you can help them.

5. **Most Aware Stage** – This is where your prospect is ready to make a purchase but hasn't yet done so for whatever reason. This is the time to WOW your prospects and really amp up the product and value of it. Focus on how this will transform their lives and what their life will look like once they have used your solution.

All prospects start at the "unaware" stage and move through the entire spectrum. When they become buyers, it's because they've been convinced enough to give you a try.

The "unaware" stage makes up the bulk of your market – and as you move through the stages, the number of people who sit on the spectrum of awareness will drastically reduce until you get to the buying stage.

Specifically, around 75–80% of people fall in the "unaware" stage, while only around 1–3% of your market are ready to buy now.

In terms of ads on Facebook for example, your market might be around one million... but by the time you get leads into your funnel, you might only have around 1,000 leads... and as they continue to move through the stages of your funnel, your actual buyers might be around 10% of the total number of leads.

At each stage of awareness, you need to educate, persuade and increase the desire for your product until it tips your prospect into becoming a paying customer. The more someone knows you, the more they trust and like you; and the more your prospects "warm up to you", the greater the likelihood of them buying from you.

This is why sales from cold traffic are always lower than sales from warm and hot traffic. This is why I'm a massive fan of content marketing and email marketing, since the more touchpoints you have with your audience, the easier it is to move them from being a total stranger into a raving fan.

The five levels of awareness will show you how to split your campaigns up when using platforms like Facebook, print media and other online and offline mediums. Of course there are always exceptions to the rule, and a really great marketing campaign can take people from "unaware" to "most aware" in one go.

A good example is webinars. You might not even know who the person delivering the webinar is, but by the time you get to the end of it, you've ended up buying from them. This is because webinars are specifically engineered to demonstrate authority and expertise and increase the know, like and trust factor. They're strategically designed to move someone from "unaware" to ready to buy.

That being said, the Market Awareness Model is pretty accurate and really helpful in getting the messaging right. A typical Facebook campaign could start with content like blog posts, case studies and other content your general audience would find helpful. You can then retarget people with follow-up content that hits the other stages of awareness.

Most people start with the "problem aware" stage because it's the one that resonates most with an ideal audience. If you start nowhere else, start here. However, don't dismiss the "unaware" stage! Facebook, YouTube, TV and general publications are all good examples of mediums through which you can really tap into the "unaware" market quite quickly.

The one thing you need to remember at ALL times is relevancy. Don't put an advert in a magazine unless you KNOW with certainty that the majority of your audience is going to be reading it.

While it's common sense, I've lost count of the number of clients I've worked with over the years who've literally wasted tens of thousands on advertising that's produced little to no results because they violated this one rule.

With TV and print media in particular, there are several reasons why most businesses struggle to make these work for them:

- No understanding of their key metrics.
- No tracking in place and therefore no direct method of measuring the performance of the campaign.
- Poor copy.
- Lack of relevancy.

We'll go into these later in this book. The main concept you need to take away, however, is that ads on TV, billboards, in national newspapers or any place where the general public will see them, fall under branding-based ads. And branding (as you'll read later) is actually very difficult to get right.

Market Awareness Exercises

Below is a series of questions to help stimulate thinking for every part of the Market Awareness Model. I highly recommend you download the accompanying worksheet for these exercises for free here: http://bit.ly/MAwareness.

Unaware Stage:

1. What kind of person is most likely to buy from you at this stage?
2. What interests your prospects the most?

Problem Aware Stage:
1. What problems do your prospects have that you can solve?
2. What will happen if your prospect doesn't solve their problem?

Solution Aware Stage:
1. What does your prospect want the most?
2. What does your prospect need to agree/understand/believe before they recognise your product is right for them?

Product Aware Stage:
1. Why is your product superior to anything else on the market (what is your USP)?
2. What objections do prospects have to buying your product?

Most Aware Stage:
1. What's the best "no-brain" offer you can give your prospect?
2. What can you do post purchase to increase the "stick" rate?

These questions will help you think about each stage of the model in a more strategic

way.

Regardless of where you sit in the Market Awareness Model, you need to determine HOW you're going to reach your audience and which mediums you're going to use. That's why I want to mention the distinction between branding and direct response advertising, since understanding the difference between the two will help you make smarter advertising decisions.

In my Mind-Hack™ Marketing workshop, I cover the Market Awareness Model in detail. You can find out more by going to: http://arfasairaiqbal.com/mindhackresources.

Branding vs Direct Response Advertising

There's a war going on in the marketing world which is all behind closed doors. It's been raging for decades and it's unlikely to fizzle out anytime soon...

And that's the war of the words. Seriously.

Since the dawn of marketing, there's always been a divide between creatives who push branding and those who stand firmly in the direct response camp. This is extremely significant for you as a business owner because it's going to directly impact your bottom line.

Branding is also known as *mass marketing* and is designed to remind your audience of your brand and your offers. The big idea behind branding is that increasing exposure to your brand means you stay top of mind for potential prospects – and this means that when people need what you have to offer, they're more likely to buy from you.

Brands such as Coca-Cola, Nike and Apple do brand-based or mass marketing, and actually, most marketing you see on TV, radio, print etc. tends to fall into this category.

However, there's a huge problem with mass marketing – aside from being difficult to successfully execute, it eats up two things: time and money.

This is because your ads need to be shown across a variety of different media for an extensive amount of time in order to get potential customers interested. Brand agencies tend to call these "saturation campaigns".

Direct response marketing, on the other hand, is a different ball game altogether. This type of marketing is designed to generate an immediate response from consumers. Moreover, unlike mass marketing, each response can be tracked and measured – and this means you can clearly attribute return on investment (ROI) to individual ads.

The Problem With Brand-Based Advertising

While branding certainly has its place, it is, in my opinion, not something the average business owner should even try to attempt. This is because brand-based marketing is largely unmeasurable.

No one ad can be attributed to bringing in the money – and this means for small business owners that money often disappears faster than a speeding bullet!

The worst part, however, is that most branding agencies will try to convince you that if your ads aren't bringing in the money, you need to INCREASE the number of ads you're running or increase the variety of media you're advertising in (and very often they will tell you to do both) to make the ads "stick" and "work".

And this means you can end up down a huge, and what can seem like a never-ending, rabbit hole of money and stress to go with it... with very few results to show for it in return.

Brands like Apple and Coca-Cola can pull off brand-based advertising because they're big enough to have huge budgets which run into the millions. And while there's no doubt these campaigns certainly work, it's rarely the case for small business owners who try to emulate the big guns.

Case in point, one of my clients decided to go ahead with a very expensive four-month-long TV campaign aimed at a niche audience on a satellite TV channel. The goal was simple: get as many people as possible registering for a free seven-day trial of a membership site.

The plan was to air the ad multiple times a day, plus sponsor one of their shows. Despite the audience being mostly the target demographic, the campaign was a complete failure.

The first month of the campaign, the results looked to be promising – but by the time week six kicked in, it was losing money – FAST.

As the weeks ticked by, it became increasingly clear the campaign was a disaster. My client raised it with the channel, who suggested they should increase the number of airtime slots – which they did (at no additional cost), but to no avail.

After spending £28,000 in the hope of generating thousands of leads, my client made a stinging £13,000 loss – a huge hole to dig yourself out of when you're only selling a £14 widget with no significant upsell!

It took 14 months of cost-cutting (including slashing employee salaries) and intense conversion optimisation on existing funnels and campaigns to recover from the damage.

Unfortunately, too many small businesses struggle with trying to emulate bigger brands – but the truth is they simply can't compete. Every market has its own challenges, which is why it's important to have a bullet-proof strategy for how you're going to grow and scale.

International brands go for market share and rapid growth by trying to penetrate as many markets as possible. They already have a ton of data to work with and have the budget and the infrastructure in place to support growth.

Smaller businesses, on the other hand, have none of these things. They simply can't compete because not only do they operate on smaller margins with higher costs relative to their giant counterparts, but they also rarely have the infrastructure (systems, processes and people) or budget to support scale.

At this point you might be wondering how you can advertise as effectively as the big guns, without the added risk.

That's where direct response marketing comes into play. How ads make money really comes down to being able to track and measure their effectiveness so you can immediately see what's working and what's not – and this is the backbone of how direct response works.

Direct Response Marketing Is Going to Become Your Best Friend

I'm a huge fan of direct response because it works for every business – regardless of size. It's how I was classically trained, and I learned very quickly that if your marketing can't be accounted for and you can't attribute ROI to your ads and campaigns, you'll practically leak money and you won't even know it.

That's the premise behind direct response. **It's the ability to get an instant reaction from the audience and measure the outcome accurately.** This means you can track every campaign and clearly see which campaigns are producing the highest number of sales.

Unlike brand-based advertising which sucks a lot of budget quickly and is slow to produce any kind of return, direct response has only two outcomes: sales or no sales – there is no middle ground or grey area. Either way, you can clearly attribute ROI to specific ads.

Direct response gives you a greater degree of control over your budget and is not only easier to implement, but highly profitable when you know your numbers. This is why direct response is my weapon of choice when implementing everything inside of *Mind-Hack™ Marketing*.

Depending on how much it costs to acquire a lead and a customer, you can scale your best-performing campaigns quickly or incrementally in stages – so nothing ever turns out as a "nasty surprise".

I once had a conversation with a client whose company had been running ads in various print magazines over the course of a few years.

Nothing was tracked, nothing was measured. My client couldn't attribute any sales directly to these ads, and worse, he'd spent in excess of £32,000 on these ads. The result? Forget sales (the average sale for him is £60,000), he didn't

get any. Not. Even. One. Single. Lead.
OUCH!

Worse still, he was completely unaware of it! It wasn't until I asked him to get me all the advertising data and leads generated that he figured out he'd made a huge loss.

This kind of money can break a small business very quickly – and if you're not careful, can literally be the death of you. Thankfully, my team and I were able to solve my client's lead-generation problem so not only was everything tracked and measured, but the leads were also producing sales profitably.

Remember what I said at the beginning of this book – more businesses go broke trying to grow than for any other reason. This is because they spend large amounts of money on advertising with the sole focus of trying to acquire new customers.

While there's nothing wrong with trying to get more customers, it's a massive problem when you can't account for your ad spend and you've no idea how much you've spent to acquire a customer. It's even worse when you can't attribute ROI to your ads.

Case in point – brand advertising rarely works for small businesses!

I've yet to meet a SINGLE small business owner who can say with certainty that they've managed to run a successful brand-based marketing campaign that resulted in positive

ROI.

Direct response marketing, on the other hand, is so much easier and more profitable for small businesses because of your ability to control everything, from the concept and ideas to the copy and even the testing and tracking of the campaign.

I'll talk more about ads later in this book, but for now, let me share some tips for writing effective campaigns. The tips below are applicable to landing pages, sales pages and ads.

1) Headline – Your ad needs something to help it stand out from the crowd. A headline should hook or pull people in so they want to continue reading. Some of the best headlines can be found in newspapers and magazines and they really do compel you to want to buy them and continue reading!

A great headline should contain a big benefit or promise and make you curious to want to know more. If you're struggling to write a great headline, use some of the angles covered in Chapter 9 to help you!

I also have free training on how to write compelling headlines available inside my Facebook group – here's the link to it: http://bit.ly/headlinetraining (you'll need to request access to the group first!).

2) Solve a problem – What's the big problem you're solving? How can you help people in solving this problem?

3) Big benefits – What are the big benefits of someone doing business with you? How will their life improve as a result?

4) Include emotional triggers where possible – Focus on the feelings you want to leave people with. Are you offering relief from stress, giving people confidence or helping people feel good?

5) A strong call to action – Tell people EXACTLY what to do next. So if you want someone to click on a button, tell them! If you want someone to call you, tell them!

If you're using these tips to help you write ads, it's important to understand what KIND of an ad you're writing – for example, if you're writing Google Ads or banner ads, it's much harder to cram all the above into just a few lines.

Each platform has its own limitations which you should be aware of – but if you're running ads in print, then you're pretty much ok.

Summary

In this chapter, we discussed how there are only three ways to grow a business and how brand-based advertising rarely works for smaller businesses. Instead, direct response marketing is the only kind of marketing you should be doing.

Key concepts we covered in this chapter include:

- Customer acquisition is one of the greatest costs in a

business and can cause a business to go bust if not done properly.

- The five levels of awareness will help you understand how to speak to your potential customers depending on how aware they are.
- Direct response marketing is trackable and can be used to scale a business incrementally AND profitably.

In the next chapter, we'll explore the wonderful world of sales funnels and how you too can plan out your first funnel.

Chapter 9: The Different Stages of a Sales Funnel

Google the term "sales funnel" and you'll get many different diagrams, explanations and process-flows back at you – it can feel pretty daunting to sift through.

Sales funnels by their very nature are often touted as the "cure all" to making money online – and that wouldn't be so far from the truth. Creating a sales funnel means ensuring you've understood your ideal client and customer journey and then mapped out a funnel that aligns with both.

What Is a Sales Funnel?

There are many different kinds of sales funnels, but regardless of the type, a sales funnel is simply a mechanism that:

- Attracts your ideal prospects into your world.
- Educates, inspires and helps your prospects with useful information and insights.
- Encourages prospects to take the next step with you (such as book a call or purchase something).

When done properly, each stage of a sales funnel is designed to increase the know, like and trust factor, warming prospects up so they're more likely to buy from you.

I should mention here that your goal shouldn't JUST be the

sale itself – rather, you want to increase a customer's lifetime value by getting them to buy from you repeatedly.

The reason why the process is referred to as a funnel is because it behaves just like a funnel. Lots of interest happens at the top of the funnel, but by the time that interest turns into actual buyers, only a very small percentage of people will have actually bought.

In its simplest form, a sales funnel consists of the following:

- An irresistible offer – a piece of valuable content that helps to solve the problem your prospect has.
- A landing page to capture the details of your ideal prospect.
- A pre-selling sequence – a series of seven emails designed to encourage your prospects to want to buy from you.
- An order page/sales page your prospects can purchase from OR a calendar scheduling page so prospects can book a call.
- Running ads to your funnel so you can attract, engage and convert your ideal prospects into paying customers.

While the process is simple, the actual development of all of these different elements is a time-consuming process and can take weeks or even months to pull together if you've never created a sales funnel before.

The HUGE advantage of a sales funnel is that it behaves like your personal salesperson who works 24/7 to attract prospects, build a relationship with them and then turn them into buyers.

A sales funnel can radically improve your efficiency as a business and skyrocket your sales in the process.

However, it can take a lot of testing and tweaking to get a great funnel up and running. This is called optimisation and we'll talk more about that later in Chapter 13.

For now, it's important to understand that a sales funnel must be viable in order to make sales successfully. This means taking a number of predetermined steps FIRST to ensure the funnels you create stand the best chance of converting before you optimise.

This has two major benefits:

- Drives down the cost of ad spend.
- Ensures you have the best chance of making the funnel profitable.

Here's what these steps look like:

1. Understand the ideal customer.
2. Create an offer relevant to the ideal customer.
3. Test the offer organically (if it doesn't work organically, it's not going to work paid).
4. Pick the perfect traffic source (where is your audience hanging out?).
5. Get the offer in front of ideal clients via paid traffic.
6. Run people through a pre-selling sequence which gets people excited to buy.
7. Send people to the sales page to either buy something OR

book a consultation with you.

We've already covered some of these in earlier chapters of this book. From this point onwards, you'll understand how to complete the entire process.

How to Plan Your Funnel

In order to plan your funnel correctly, it's important to first understand the three different stages of a funnel:

1. Top of Funnel
2. Middle of Funnel
3. Bottom of Funnel.

Stage 1: Top of Funnel (also known as ToFu) – Designed to generate interest from your target market into actual leads on your list and involves:

- Building awareness and interest in how you solve problems for prospects.
- High-value content, including social media posts.
- Lead-generating activities such as running paid ads, webinars etc.
- Using an irresistible offer such as a lead magnet (see below).
- Tripwires are a great way to help liquidate the cost of your ads at this stage (more about this later).
- The question prospects are asking at this stage of the funnel process is, *"What do I need to solve my problem?"*

Lead Magnets and Tripwires

A lead magnet is the first touchpoint in your funnel that involves your prospect giving you their details in exchange for valuable content. Lead magnets have many names, including an "irresistible offer", "opt-in offer", "ethical bribe" and "sign-up offer", to name a few.

A great lead magnet solves ONE problem for ONE ideal customer – in other words, get really specific about how you can help your ideal prospect. If you promise to solve too many things in your lead magnet, it won't work because it will usually take too long or become too complicated to implement.

The golden rule is to keep things easy and simple – one big promise where the payoff is really valuable for the prospect. Even better, a great lead magnet should be something valuable enough to charge money for – but you aren't charging!

A big tip is to have lead magnets that are quick and easy to consume. Anything that takes more than 30 minutes to get through is too long and needs to be reconsidered. The perfect lead magnet will also share the WHAT and some of the HOW – enough to get prospects started, but not enough to give them the complete solution.

I like to think of lead magnets as being the "starters" in a restaurant – they should be good enough to whet your appetite and make you hungry for more!

A great landing page has five key elements at the bare minimum:

1. Attention-grabbing headline.
2. Details of your free offer, including the USP and the main benefits.
3. Social proof such as testimonials, reviews, video testimonials, etc.
4. Call to action (such as "Download Now").
5. A hero image (showing the end result/outcome) of the thing you are offering.

Your USP or unique selling point can be woven into the headline and the offer and you can even reference it again just before your call to action.

The number one thing you need to remember with a landing page is that your prospect should ONLY be able to take the action you want them to (for example, sign up) or leave.

Do NOT include links to the rest of your website on your landing page because it's distracting, and people can easily forget why they landed on your page in the first place.

Lead magnets include things like reports, PDF guides, tools, checklists, templates, quizzes, consultations, demos/free trials, white papers etc.

A successful lead magnet should seed your main product/ offer and should not only get prospects excited, but should also build desire for your prospects to want to "ascend" to the next level with you – which can be a tripwire offer or the main product.

Tripwires, meanwhile, are valuable pieces of content that also solve a problem just like lead magnets – but you usually ask prospects to pay for them. Some tripwires don't require money, but DO require an investment of time (such as X day challenges, mini workshops and webinars).

Paid tripwires are designed to:

- Liquidate (or cover) the cost of your ad spend.
- Increase the number of customers you have.
- Pre-qualify prospects for your higher-priced solutions.
- Help you grow a list of buyers, which can be worth up to 50 times more than a list of non-buyers (depending on the niche).

Tripwires are usually offered immediately after a lead magnet – and are a brilliant way to separate your list between people who are more likely to continue buying from you and those who are less likely to buy from you.

Stage 2: Middle of Funnel (also known as MoFu) – Once a lead has opted into your funnel, the middle of the funnel is all about nurturing leads and engaging with prospects and customers:

- Use the middle of the funnel to deliver content that both educates and gives clarity to prospects about the problem they have.

- At this stage, email sequences should nurture and pre-sell prospects on the right solution for them.
- The middle of the funnel is also your chance to position your offer or signature system as THE solution for your prospects.
- The question prospects are asking at this stage of the funnel process is, *"Why do I need the solution from you?"*

Email marketing is essential to making the middle of the funnel work efficiently. We'll talk more about email marketing later in the book.

Stage 3: Bottom of Funnel (also known as BoFu) – This stage is about customer acquisition and ascension (getting customers to buy more from you or buy higher-priced offerings):

- You must explain why your product is the best solution for your prospect.
- Pricing and offer are critical, since your prospect is making a buying decision.
- At this stage, you would include a sales page/video/pitch for your signature system.
- This stage may also involve getting prospects onto a sales call.
- Around 1–3% of your market is ready to buy right now.
- The question prospects are asking at this stage of the funnel process is, *"Why should I buy the solution right now?"*
- BoFu is also the stage where you reactivate past clients and encourage repeat purchases.
- This stage usually includes upsells or ascending customers

to the next logical stage in their journey.

Your job is to ensure you create a smooth transition from the top of the funnel all the way to the bottom of the funnel, so buying feels easy and the right thing to do.

At the very start of a prospect's journey with you, it's essential the top of the funnel inspires, motivates and compels your audience into your sales funnel – in other words, to get people's name, email and other personal data.

By the time you get to the bottom of the funnel, not only do you want people to buy, you want them to buy from you repeatedly. When done correctly, your funnel should help to increase the lifetime value of a customer.

By the way, if you need help with creating your own sales funnel, check out https://funnelinabox.co.uk/ where my incredible team and I will build your entire funnel for you.

The Power of Upsells/Ascension

Ascending or upselling customers to the next logical stage is something you want to make as easy and as effortless as possible.

One of the best examples is this: *"Would you like fries with that?"*

Six power-packed words that have been responsible for over $19.21bn in revenue in 2020 for one of the best-known franchises in the world – McDonald's[13].

The real power of McDonald's and its fortune lies in the power of the upsell. An upsell simply means getting your customer to make a higher-cost purchase than they originally planned – in other words, an upgrade.

By simply offering an additional product/service at the point of sale, you can dramatically improve your revenue with little effort on your part.

Downselling and Cross-Selling

It's worth mentioning downsells and cross-sells at this point. Sometimes, there may not be an upsell to offer customers. Other times, customers might not be interested in an upsell or might not even be interested in the main offer.

Rather than lose the sale entirely, a downsell can be offered instead. In my own business, if clients turn down my main proposal, I usually offer a smaller version of the proposal instead at a lower price point.

Cross-selling is where you offer your customers something different (but complementary) to your purchase. Amazon is a great example of using cross-selling. If you buy a lamp from Amazon as an example, then Amazon will show you bulbs to go with the lamp.

---

[13] (2021), 'Revenue of the McDonald's Corporation worldwide from 2005 to 2020', Statista, February, available at: https://www.statista.com/statistics/208917/revenue-of-the-mcdonalds-corporation-since-2005/

Here are some ideas to get you started with upsells, downsells and cross-sells:

- Offer the customer something complementary to the original purchase e.g. pens with paper at a higher price point.
- Offer an upsell that solves a problem created by the original purchase e.g. ask people to buy training with a purchase of software.
- Position an upsell as a "no-brainer" offer that costs less than the original item e.g. you buy a dress and need the perfect bag to go with it at a bargain price.
- People pay for speed of execution which is perfect for service-based businesses. Can you offer something that saves time or money or allows your customers to get a result faster?
- Offer customers smaller-scale versions of a product as a downsell.

One of the best funnels I personally went through was Frank Kern's book funnel – it was pretty epic. Frank Kern is considered to be one of the best marketing consultants on the planet.

From what I can recall (it was several years ago), I bought one of Frank's books from an advert on Facebook. After I bought the book, I signed up for his book funnel workshop (a tripwire because it required a whole day of my time) and I sat through the whole thing.

Throughout the workshop, Frank pitched his Inner Circle

membership programme for $297/month. He pitched several times, each time layering on more bonuses and, in the end, I signed up and STAYED on his Inner Circle for two years.

As a side note, book funnels are brilliant if you're an expert. I've personally gone through several of them and ended up buying the tripwire, the core product and the upsell too.

Funnel Planning

The best way to plan your funnel is to figure out what your prospects need and then deliver a solution to them based on this need. The way I like to think of it is this: there's a gap between where your avatar is and where they want to be — and the opportunity to sell and serve someone exists in this gap.

Planning your funnel means understanding the problems your avatar is experiencing and then breaking the funnel down to fill the gap. A great lead magnet and tripwire will help CREATE a gap for the next product because, essentially, you're deliberately holding back information that can help the client solve their entire problem.

The prospect would therefore need to buy the upsell or core product in order to get a complete solution to their problem.

Specifically, there are two ways you can plan your funnel:

- Focus on the problems you can help solve for your avatar if you don't yet have a product, and develop your offers accordingly.

- If you already have a product, you can reverse engineer it by breaking it down, so you understand which problems it solves for your avatar. This may involve breaking off parts of your core product and selling/offering them as a lead magnet and tripwire.

Exercise: Planning Your Funnel

Here's an exercise to help you plan your funnel:

1. Write down all the problems your avatar has in relation to your product/service.
2. What solution can you offer for each problem?
3. Identify what your lead magnet, tripwire, core product and upsell or ascension offer could be in order to help move your prospect from becoming a lead to becoming a paying customer and then a repeat customer.

For example, if you sell a weight loss product and your avatar is a busy professional who is short on time, here's how I would plan the funnel:

Problem	Solution
No time to exercise	Short workouts of just 5-10 minutes
No time to cook	10-minute meals
No time to meal plan	10-minute meal planning + shopping list

Now identify your offers for every stage of the funnel – remember, each part of the funnel needs to create and fill a gap in your prospect's understanding and create the desire for the next element.

Funnel Step	Offer
Lead Magnet	5 Ways to Flatten Your Abs in Just 5 Minutes
Tripwire	10 Easy 10-minute Weight Loss Recipes
Core Offer	90-Day Total Body Makeover
Ascension	Fit Forever Monthly Subscription

Tips to Create Compelling Offers

I've worked with countless clients who have not managed to make their funnel work for many different reasons – one of them being that the offers themselves are simply not compelling enough for prospects.

How you name your offers matters!

A "keep fit" guide is going to be a hard lead magnet to push compared to "5 Ways to Flatten Your Abs in Just 5 Minutes" because it's too vague. There's no big promise or payoff and prospects don't know what to expect.

"5 Ways to Flatten Your Abs in Just 5 Minutes" is compelling because it's:

- Super specific
- Offers a big promise
- Solves one problem.

The title implies the lead magnet is super quick and easy to complete, plus promises to flatten your abs.

A few formulas you can use to help you write compelling headlines include:

1. How to X (benefit) Without Y (pain point).
2. X (number) Ways to Y (result).
3. X (number) Tips to Y (pain point you want to resolve).

Lastly, visuals, videos, infographics and a nice clean layout with plenty of white space will really help your lead magnet get consumed.

Your First Sales Funnel

So far we've covered the different stages of a sales funnel and have also talked about planning your funnel. The question I often get asked is which kind of funnel should I get started with?

Whenever I work with a business that's just getting started with digital marketing, one of the first funnels I ever create for them is what I call the Quick Launch Funnel.

The Quick Launch Funnel is basically a one-page business model that's a really simple way to help you launch a product or a programme FAST! Other marketers might call this an opt-in or lead-magnet funnel – of all the funnel types that exist, it's actually the easiest one to implement.

Since 2010, I've created hundreds of these for one reason and one reason alone – it WORKS. It works because of its sheer simplicity and effectiveness in making money quickly.

Unlike other sales funnels that can be time-consuming and complicated to execute, the Quick Launch Funnel is so easy to set up that you only really need three things to get started:

- **An opt-in landing page** – You don't even need a website as most email autoresponder providers have plenty of landing page templates you can use.

- **Email autoresponder provider** – You can use something basic like GetResponse, Aweber, ConvertKit, MailerLite etc., or more sophisticated systems like Kartra, KEAP, GrooveFunnels and Clickfunnels etc. to deliver your emails.
- **Ability for your prospects to buy or book a call** – Link to your sales page/order page OR a link to your calendar.

And that's pretty much it!

As an overview, here's what this would look like:

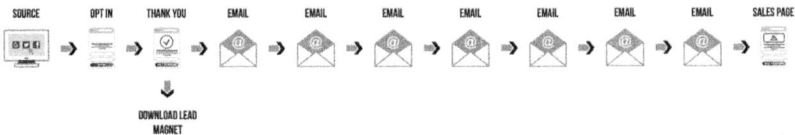

As you can see, there's nothing complicated here. Traffic flows to a landing page so prospects can opt in and download a lead magnet, before being pushed to a series of seven strategically written emails and a sales/order page or a calendar booking link.

There are many different funnel types you can run, such as webinar funnels, quiz funnels, video sales letter funnels etc., but in all honesty, they are a LOT more complex to create and set up.

We'll talk more about email marketing and sales pages later in the book, but for now, you should have everything you need to understand the basics.

If you'd like help with creating your own sales funnel with guidance and support, I have a three-day bootcamp where I teach you how to build your own client-attracting funnel from scratch. Simply go to http://arfasairaiqbal.com/mindhackresources to learn more.

Summary

In this chapter, we covered the three different stages of a funnel which are:

- Top of Funnel – attracting the right prospects to become leads.
- Middle of Funnel – nurturing and pre-selling leads.
- Bottom of Funnel – turning leads into customers and repeat customers.

We covered lead magnets, tripwires, upsells, downsells and cross-sells and also talked about how you plan the stages of a funnel to include these elements.

Lastly, I shared with you the Quick Launch Funnel – so called because of all the different funnel types that exist, it's by far the easiest to implement and get results from.

In the next chapter, I'm going to dig deeper into direct response advertising and share the inside secrets of how to write highly persuasive and compelling copy.

By the way, if you need help with building your funnel, check out the resources section at the end of the book.

Chapter 10: Direct Response Advertising

Earlier in this book, I talked about the difference between brand-based advertising and direct response, and why direct response is the only choice if you're a small business looking to profit from advertising. I also shared some tips on how to use direct response in your marketing.

In this chapter, I want to delve a little deeper into direct response advertising strategies. From ad creatives to storytelling, I'll be sharing powerful insights from over a decade of writing highly responsive ads for clients, as well as my top tips and secrets for writing high-converting ads that will practically crush your competition.

Let's get straight to it!

The Goal of Advertising

The goal of advertising is to make money. It's a method of finding customers for your business. So, for every £1 you spend, you get at least £2 or more back in order for it to be profitable.

When you've figured out how to turn £1 into £2 predictably and consistently, you now have something that can be scaled. This is how businesses can grow quickly, easily and, more importantly, profitably.

This is critical if you're looking to scale, because sadly too many businesses run ads at a loss and don't even know it.

Typical conversion rates online are between 1% and 10% depending on your business...

Most businesses fall under 4%, which means that **for every 100 people who stop by your website, around 96 of them are falling through the cracks** – and this is pretty worrying, especially if you've paid good money to get traffic to your website in the first place. That's a BIG problem and it's costing you a LOT of money...

Worse, if you don't have a system in place that converts leads into buyers and repeat buyers, you may as well be burning cold, hard cash! I'm NOT a fan of getting the WRONG leads on your list...

Because if a lead isn't making you money, it's COSTING you money.

Aside from having a really good product and offer, here's what you need to do in order to run ads profitably:

- Figure out your ideal customer so when you build your list, it's QUALIFIED (in other words, the RIGHT people are on your list).
- Write copy that speaks to the pain points of your end user.
- Ensure that your landing pages can be carefully tracked.
- Have a customised user journey to convert leads into buyers.

We'll go into ads later in the book, but for now, let me walk you through an example where you are selling a £10 widget to an UNQUALIFIED group of people:

- You spend £100 to get 100 people to your ad.
- 10 people opt in to your list, which is a 10% conversion rate and the cost per lead is £10.
- Now let's say you stick these 10 people into a sequence to sell your stuff and two people buy a £10 widget.
- This means only 2% of people who saw your ad actually bought from you.
- They paid you £20, but you spent £100 to get those sales, and that means you're now running at an £80 loss.

Most business owners think that the problem is they need more eyeballs on their offer – so they'll throw more money at it in the hope they can make it work. In reality, they're only speeding up their failure.

If the numbers don't work with 100 people, they are NOT going to work with 1,000 people!!

Now imagine you're marketing to a QUALIFIED group of people (your ideal customers) and your copy/messaging in your lead generation system is tailored to them.

Here's an example of what the numbers look like now:

- You spend £100 to get 100 people to your ad.
- 30 people opt in to your list, which is a 30% conversion rate and the cost per lead is £3.33.

- Now let's say you stick these 30 people into a TAILORED sequence to sell your stuff and 20 people buy a £10 widget.
- This means 20% of people who saw your ad actually bought from you.
- They paid you £200, but you spent £100 to get those sales, and that means you're now running at a £100 profit.

Your aim is to basically put £1 in and get £2 or more out!

And when the numbers work, you can start SCALING and growing your business!

Now, these metrics are super important for you to be tracking like clockwork – and if you can't track them, you should NOT be running ads – period.

You need to know that for every £1 you spend on ads, you're getting at LEAST £2 out. I've lost count of the number of business owners who run ads without any clear understanding of the metrics and then wonder why they go broke.

As I've mentioned previously in this book, more businesses go broke trying to grow than for any other reason. Investopedia[14] recently reported that more than 90% of startups fail.

90% is an insane number! That means out of every 10 people who start a business, only one will make it work. There are lots of reasons why startups fail – and poor or ineffective

---

[14] Sean Bryant, "How Many Startups Fail and Why?", Investopedia, 9 November 2020, available at: https://www.investopedia.com/articles/personal-finance/040915/how-many-startups-fail-and-why.asp

marketing is one of them.

If you don't have a predictable, consistent and measurable way of collecting leads and turning them into paying customers and repeat customers, then the statistics are clear: your business has a high probability of failing.

Here's the other thing – and this is something most businesses tend to miss – the cost of ad management.

If you have someone who is running the ads FOR you, then you also need to account for their costs too – and this means you could end up STILL running at a loss.

Some businesses may run at a loss when acquiring their initial leads, but because they have a proper machine or system in place, the leads have the potential to become customers and repeat customers.

Therefore, despite losing money on the front-end, in the long run, you MAKE many times what you spent to acquire the leads in the first place.

This is known as **ROAS or "return on ad spend"**.

So, this brings me to the question: **How can you make money from your ads?**

Understanding how ads make money is a great place to start because, in order to become profitable, you really need to ensure you're sticking to some basic rules.

As I mentioned before, the minimum you need is a way to track and measure the performance of your ads. If you can't do either, you shouldn't be running them!

Direct response legend Clayton Makepeace[15] said that, at the very least, ads MUST:

1) **Create or intensify the consumer's desire and sense of urgency to buy the product** by focusing on the benefits it will bring to the prospect.
2) **Present compelling reasons why the product is unique** and therefore superior to similar products out there, so it becomes the natural and obvious choice to prospects.
3) **Provide a way for the prospect to purchase the product at the earliest opportunity.**

Writing a successful ad takes skill – which is why copywriters not only charge a LOT of money to write them, but in many cases, take a cut of the sales too. Not to worry, even if you're not a copywriter, you can still churn out really good ads as long as you follow a few guidelines.

Different Kinds of Ad Copy

One of the key questions clients ask all the time is whether there are any perfect frameworks or templates for their ad campaigns. There are three approaches I tend to use, depending on the market:

---

[15] Clayton Makepeace, "The Total Package", now archived, available at: https://web. archive.org/web/20200401191400/http://www.makepeacetotalpackage.com/

1.   AIDA
2.   PAS
3.   Storytelling

AIDA is the perfect ad formula when entering an unknown market. That's because when you first enter or start advertising in a new market, people won't have a clue who you are.

And this creates a trust problem and "ad blindness" where people just ignore your ads. How you position yourself in a new market really means the difference between a campaign that works and one that fails.

That's why using AIDA is excellent, since it's designed to work with what people want (rather than what they are trying to solve). AIDA stands for Attention, Interest, Desire and Action:

1. **Attention** – Here's where you grab the attention of your ideal audience with curiosity, insight or something that "hooks" them into wanting to find out more about what you offer or do. Strong headlines and a powerful creative + fantastic copy are all needed here!

2. **Interest** – Create interest by sharing relevant information that's useful to your audience and keeps them reading to learn more.

3. **Desire** – Build desire by focusing on what your ideal prospect wants the most and how your product/service achieves this. You need to get people excited by focusing

on the results or transformation you offer.

4. **Action** – Once you've built the desire and got people excited, it's time to ask them to make some kind of commitment, such as buy something, download something or sign up for something – so tell them exactly what they need to do next. Be specific and don't assume they automatically know what to do!

Case studies and stories are perfect examples of the kinds of campaigns you can run using the AIDA formula to an unknown audience.

It's very much like magazines and newspapers whose entire business model is based on selling sensational stories – and the Attention comes from the killer headlines they use to hook their readers.

PAS is the perfect ad formula for an audience that is already problem aware. PAS basically stands for Problem, Agitate, Solution and looks like this:

1. **Problem** – What's the problem your ideal prospects are facing?
2. **Agitate** – What happens if they don't solve the problem?
3. **Solution** – What's your solution and what does the prospect have to do next in order to get the solution?

The PAS formula is one of my favourite formulas of all time and I use this for ALL my marketing materials – from landing pages and sales pages to emails, webinars and more.

Last but not least, ***storytelling is a fantastic framework to use for ad copy*** – and even better, it's easy to use. Storytelling is a powerful medium for attracting attention for several reasons, but more importantly, it cuts through the noise online because people are hard-wired to respond to stories.

From an evolutionary perspective, stories were how people passed on valuable lessons to other members of a community and from one generation to another. Plus, everyone loves a great story!

It's the perfect "non-salesy" approach to connecting emotionally with your audience. A great story can help people understand why your product or service works really well without the "hard sell".

A great story allows your audience to see themselves in your story and emotionally connect with you – and as I've mentioned several times throughout this book, people buy on emotion and justify with logic.

Therefore, stories are the perfect way to connect with someone on an emotional level because they speak to the subconscious mind. You can use stories to overcome objections so selling becomes easy.

You don't want people just reading your story and thinking "that's a great story" and then doing nothing. That's why, for ads, sharing your story needs to be combined with a direct call to action.

In Chapter 12, I'll cover a more detailed framework on how to sell with stories. For now, it's worth knowing that stories can be used in every element of your marketing – from your ads, emails and sales pages to videos, webinars and everything else in between.

Regardless of which kind of framework you use for your ad copy, ALL of the frameworks I've shared with you are super flexible because they can be tailored to suit your business and the product/service you're selling. As long as your copy contains all the elements of the framework you're using, you should be ok.

If you need more help with pulling your campaigns together, then the Mind-Hack™ Marketing workshop is a great place to start. To find out more, simply go to: http://arfasairaiqbal.com/mindhackresources.

Ad Creatives

While ad copy is the single most important element of any advert, ad creatives follow close behind. The wrong creative can kill your ad completely, but the right one can dramatically boost your conversion rates.

Specifically, there are seven kinds of image that routinely outperform other images – for a very interesting reason!

As Drew Eric Whitman noted in his book *Ca$hvertising*[16], Gallup conducted a poll of over 29,000 readers of 20 different Sunday papers and found that the images readers most preferred were (in order):

1. Babies and kids
2. Mothers and babies
3. Groups of adults
4. Animals
5. Sports scenes
6. Celebrities
7. Food.

The reason why these images outperformed other images is simple – they all highlight the primary and secondary human needs for:

- Love and protection
- Nurture and attention
- Family
- Social acceptance
- Social status
- The drive to win
- Food and drink.

Use these kinds of images when creating ads or any other kind of marketing collateral and see how this improves your conversion rates. You should definitely notice an improvement in your metrics compared to the same ads that do NOT use these images.

---

[16] Drew Eric Whitman, (2008), Ca$hvertising: How to Use More than 100 Secrets of Ad-agency Psychology to Make Big Money Selling Anything to Anyone, Career Press, 1st edition

Ad Tracking

Finally, ensure your ads are trackable. There are several ways you can do this. Online, you can create separate landing pages for every ad in order to track conversions accurately. Every campaign should have its own landing page so there's no confusion over where the traffic comes from.

It goes without saying that if you're using Facebook ads, the Facebook conversion API will really help with your tracking data. However, if you're a complete technophobe or new to tracking and want to get your feet wet, then using a link tracker such as bit.ly is better than nothing.

The other way you can track ads is using Google Tag Manager. Google Tag Manager essentially shows you what happens after a customer clicks on your ads – for example, did they purchase something, download something or take another action?

In print, ensure you give people a code to quote so you can attribute the ad to any revenue coming in. If your call to action is for people to call you, you can also have a separate trackable phone number.

Video Ads

I feel video ads need a special mention.

YouTube, Facebook and any other platform that uses video ads, do all require a bit more thought. That's because in many instances, you literally only have five seconds or less to grab someone's attention.

Let's take YouTube as an example. YouTube ads run at the very start of a video, but the ads have a five-second window before allowing viewers to skip the video. Therefore, you must make those five seconds count!

So let me share with you my **5P Video Ad Formula™** that I use with clients to get excellent click-through rates with video ads:

- **Punch** – Grabs people's attention based on what they want or what they don't want and makes it super punchy.
- **Positioning** – Who are you and how do you help people?
- **Problem** – Mention the problem.
- **Promise** – What's your solution?
- **Payoff** – How can people get your solution?

As long as you get the PUNCH into the first five seconds of your ad, you've already won half the battle with keeping people's attention. The ideal length for a video on YouTube is actually 15–30 seconds long on a pre-roll ad (ads before the start of a video).

Therefore, you need to ensure your ENTIRE video ad is 30 seconds long or less in order to capitalise on the ads themselves.

Here's an example of the 5P Video Ad Formula™ in action:

- **Punch** – "Never waste money on ads that don't work again."
- **Positioning** – "I'm Arfa Iqbal, eight-figure copywriter helping coaches and consultants to scale their business to their first or next seven figures."
- **Problem** – "If you're burning through ad spend..."
- **Promise** – "I've got the perfect guide to running ads that make money, so you stay profitable."
- **Payoff** – "Just click the link here to get your free guide."

Remember, you ONLY have a very small window of a prospect's attention. That means everything you say has to be super tight with no room for error or waffling, or the ads won't work. As you can see, if you run through this example, the ad is less than 30 seconds long.

Long Copy vs Short Copy – Which Is Better?

Since ads began, there's always been a divide between long copy and short copy. I've been copywriting since 2010 and, from my own experience, I can tell you that long copy routinely outperforms short copy – period. Not only does longer copy hold your audience's attention, it also builds the know, like and trust factor (more about that shortly).

David Ogilvy, who is considered to be the father of modern-day advertising, said:

"Direct response advertisers KNOW that short copy doesn't

sell. In split-run tests, long copy invariably outsells short copy."[17]

You may well disagree, but let's think about this logically for a moment. Imagine you're about to purchase a car: would you see just one ad in a magazine and buy the car?

I highly doubt it! Instead, I'm willing to bet you'd:

- Read as many reviews as possible.
- Watch YouTube videos on the performance.
- Read the brochure about the specs of the car.
- Read articles or posts from motor enthusiasts.
- Compare the car to other similar cars in its class.
- Get insights from trusted sources like Auto Trader and Top Gear.
- Maybe speak to people who own said car.
- Visit a car showroom and speak to a sales rep.
- Maybe even take the car for a test drive.

I don't know about you, but I did MOST of the above before I got my car – AND I spent MONTHS researching before I decided to go for it. If that wasn't enough, I even sent my brother who buys and sells cars to go and check the car out before I took the plunge.

In other words, I did a ton of reading and research BEFORE I made a buying decision.

---

[17] David Ogilvy, (2007), Ogilvy on Advertising, Welbeck Publishing, 1st edition

Your audience is no different. If you sell anything that might be a "considered purchase", at the very least your audience is highly likely to:

- Research
- Look for reviews and testimonials
- Compare with competitors.

It can often take days, weeks or even months before they make a buying decision. This is precisely the reason why long copy outperforms short copy. The more information a prospect has about your product, the greater the chance they will buy from you.

More information satisfies the know, like and trust factor – a crucial component in making buying decisions. The only time it won't is if you're selling an impulse purchase or if the copy is boring, fluffy or uninspiring.

As a general rule of thumb, the more expensive the purchase, the MORE copy you need. Depending on the product, your prospects may well need to jump on a lengthy sales call with a sales rep before deciding to buy.

And if you're entering the market with a brand-new product, you'd be surprised at how much copy is actually needed to sell it.

The Five Most Powerful Words in the English Language
Writing ad copy is a real art – and in fact, when writing ANY copy, you need to understand which words will get your

audience to pay more attention to you.

Specifically, there are *five* super-powerful words that are highly persuasive and can dramatically improve your conversion rates.

Here they are:

1) **Free**

Who doesn't love free stuff? From a psychological point of view, free means prospects feel they are gaining something, and not taking advantage triggers the fear of missing out.

The caveat here is that free can also attract a lot of tyre-kickers or people who love to waste your time and don't value what you do.

2) **Because**

This one might surprise you, but study after study has found that using the word "because" to explain why you are doing something will increase response rates – even if the reason you give isn't a massively compelling reason.

So when selling your stuff, use the word "because" to explain the features and benefits of what you're offering. It's a subtle way of nudging people towards a "yes".

3) **You**

This is one of the highest converting words you can use in copy. People are only ever interested in themselves and what's in it for them. Using the word "you" makes your copy instantly more relevant to your ideal customer because it speaks directly to them.

One EASY tweak you can make to your web copy, for example, is to change ALL the instances of "I" or "We" to "You", like this...

Example: "We've got 20 years' experience."

Becomes: "With 20 years of experience behind us, you can rest assured we know what we're doing!"

4) **New**

This might seem a little strange, but the word "new" implies it's never been seen before. People LOVE new things as they have the novelty factor. It also makes people curious because they like things that they perceive to be better than the original.

That being said, use "new" with caution – especially if you have a popular product that you are reformulating to make a "new" improved version of it.

For example, I used to love Maybelline's SuperStay foundation – but when they released a NEW version of it, I absolutely hated it and just wanted them to bring back the old formula. So be careful, because "new" doesn't always mean better!

5) Instantly

This is a great word to use because people are impatient creatures and we want things NOW. So any product/service that can give instant results is always going to be a winner. Instant implies speed to solution and people will pay to get results faster.

Lowering the Cost of Your Ads in Facebook

Ad costs can make or break a business. The businesses that win are the ones that can spend the most to acquire a customer and STILL be in profit. The question then inevitably revolves around lowering the cost of your ads so you get the best ROI you possibly can.

With Facebook ads, there are six elements that you can tweak to reduce the cost of your ads – these are as follows:

1. **Market** – We've already covered this in a LOT of detail throughout this book. Testing different audiences (including "lookalike audiences" in Facebook, where Facebook will go and find more people who are similar to your existing audience), will help you lower your ad costs. You're looking for audiences with high intent so they're most likely to respond to your ads.

   A ninja trick is to separate each and every single audience

into multiple ad sets that are broken down by gender, age, location and interests. By getting super granular with the demographics, you can then switch off the lowest performing ad sets to find the most profitable audiences.

2. **Message** – Once you know your market, the messaging becomes much easier. Remember what I said earlier: people buy on emotion and justify with logic. Therefore, speak to the emotions of the reader. The caveat here is that at the time of writing this book, Facebook has clamped down on the use of "you" and "your" in ads and also clamped down on speaking to the audience directly. Therefore, if you can, write ads from a personal perspective and tell your story without saying your audience is struggling/experiencing the same.

3. **Medium** – It's just as important to know what medium your audience prefers so you can create content/ads and offers that use the right medium. For example, hairdressers are not known to be heavy readers, so offering a book aimed at them would likely be a waste of time. A video, on the other hand, may well be more appealing and more likely to be consumed.

4. **Relevancy** – Your audience is struggling with many things, but the best campaigns tap into the pain points or desires your audience REALLY cares about. The more relevant the ad, the greater the chance of success. Ads with high relevance (scoring at LEAST a seven or more inside Facebook's ad manager under the "Relevancy" column) will cost less than ads that are less relevant.

5. **Frequency** – The number of times your ad copy is shown across the Facebook platform is going to impact the cost of the ads. The higher the frequency, the higher the ad cost. According to Facebook, you're looking for a frequency below 3.4, because any higher and the ad loses its effectiveness.

   Ideally, you want to combine high relevancy with low frequency to really drive down the cost of your ads.

6. **Creative** – Be willing to test lots of creatives! Find images that stand out and get you to notice the ad – and no, they don't necessarily have to be relevant to what you're offering.

   The caveat here is that if you're selling something physical, then you absolutely SHOULD show images of your product. Be prepared to use "off-brand" colours in your creatives to see what works best. Test copy with multiple creatives to find the winning combination.

As a side note, be aware that if you can't get your ads to work and you start testing different elements, test the images and the headlines first since they are the easiest to test.

ALWAYS test one thing at a time so you know what worked and what didn't.

Summary

In this chapter, we covered ads and the principles behind

effective advertising. Specifically, here's what we discussed:

- If the numbers don't work when testing ads with a smaller budget, they will never work with a larger budget.
- The AIDA framework is the perfect ad framework for reaching new markets, while the PAS formula works really well for existing markets.
- Storytelling is an excellent way to write ads that connect emotionally with ideal prospects.
- There are many things that impact the effectiveness of ads – from the word choice and headlines to the creatives and even the length of the copy.
- Long copy routinely outperforms short copy.

In the next chapter, I'll be sharing one of my favourite frameworks ever – it's called the **Continual Sales Loop™** and shows you how to sell one product to your list many times, without burning your list out.

Chapter 11: The Continual Sales Loop™

You may have noticed recently that email isn't what it used to be. Open rates are lower, click-through rates have reduced and, overall, people seem less engaged than normal...

In fact, if you follow any big-name marketer, you may have even heard them talk about the "death of email".

While it seems depressing, the good news is it's also a huge opportunity. Because when done right, email is, in my opinion, an awesome way to make more money because an email list is an asset that you OWN.

However, the caveat is you MUST be nurturing your list appropriately. If you're in the habit of emailing your list once in a blue moon with random offers and not much else, you're definitely doing it wrong.

It's a bit like this:

Imagine walking into a supermarket to buy some bread...

As you walk through the door, a salesperson enthusiastically offers some new fragrance for you to try, and you politely say no...

A few moments later, the same person comes to you again and offers you the same product. Again you say no....

Just as you're about to approach the bread aisle, there they are again! Waving that same bottle of smelly stuff in your face and asking you to try!

This time, not only do you want to tell this person to leave you alone, but you're so annoyed, you leave and go elsewhere to buy your bread...

On reflection, even a complete marketing novice would say this is a terrible way to pitch a product – yet this is EXACTLY what most businesses do to their prospects when they send them email after email asking them to buy their stuff!

Peddling the same product and offer to your list repeatedly can lead to:

- Low engagement
- High opt-out rates
- High spam complaints
- Low sales – if any!

If this is what you're currently doing, you need to stop. This kind of selling will only hurt your business in the long run and cost you dearly. In fact, it's one of the reasons why some email service providers shut down accounts or negatively impact your email deliverability rate.

Here's what works instead: RELEVANCY!

If you haven't figured it out by now, relevancy is one of the core drivers of the entire Mind-Hack™ Marketing process.

The number one tip to solving your email woes is to stay relevant. Sounds obvious, and it is, but you'd be surprised at the number of businesses that really mess this up.

You need to figure out the pain points, problems, desires, fears, dreams and motivations of your ideal customers and use this information to write about the things that matter to them most. Good job we've already covered this in the first part of this book!

If you can do this and do it consistently, you've won 80% of the battle with email.

Tip number two is to be consistent. Email regularly and at least once a week if you can so people don't forget who you are. This is important! People are busy and if you don't stay top of mind, they'll forget about you.

My third tip is to focus on your customers and not yourself. If all you do is talk about yourself and your business, you'll irritate people and they'll disengage. Customers only care about themselves, so focus on them as much as possible!

Last tip: give value first wherever you can! Share the good stuff and be generous with it. Share tips, resources, blog posts, videos and other awesome content. A good rule of thumb is the 80/20 rule: 80% of the time, be sharing content; 20% of the time, make offers.

And actually, if you do it right, you can technically make offers in every single email you write – but there's an art to it, and it ALL starts with understanding who your ideal customer is.

If you want to use email effectively in your business and want to start making more money from it, then you need to get smart about how you make offers to your list.

By changing up the angles you use to put content out in your email, you dramatically lessen the likelihood of irritating your list. I call this process the Continual Sales Loop™. This is where I'll show you no fewer than 29 different ways to sell the SAME product to your list without burning it out.

I'll cover this in detail shortly, but for now, I want to give you a high-level overview to show you why this works. I'll also be sharing some of my best tips on making email work for you in this chapter as well.

Let's dive in!

How to Sell More of Your Products WITHOUT Burning Out Your List!

There's a right way and a wrong way to make multiple offers to your list. The wrong way is to sell, sell, sell or repeatedly share the same message with your audience.

Sadly, this is exactly what ends up happening with many businesses that end up getting stuck in a rut and churning out the same old stuff repeatedly. This irritates and burns out your list, increasing dissatisfaction and almost begging for your audience to hit the unsubscribe button.

So what's the RIGHT way to make the SAME offer to your list multiple times?

Here's how to do it:

Step 1 – Identify your avatar.
Step 2 – Identify your personas.
Step 3 – Create your angles.
Step 4 – Start making offers.

The formula for the number of offers you can make to your list without irritating them is basically:

A x A = O

total number of avatars and personas x number of angles = number of offers you can make to your list

Number of Avatars/Personas	Number of Angles	Number of Offers You Make To Your List
3	10	30
3	15	45
3	29	87
4	29	116

In the table above, you can see just how powerful a concept this truly is. If you had four avatars and personas in total and 29 ad angles, you could EASILY make 116 offers to your list. And that's just with ONE product!

The more angles you have, the more offers you can make. The trick to getting this to work is to wrap your offers in good content (it could be a story, a resource, tips, advice, videos... anything you want!) BEFORE you make an offer.

I call this process the Continual Sales Loop™ and it's the best way to make multiple offers to your list without annoying them (because, let's face it, hammering your list with the same offer repeatedly only ticks off your subscribers, who just unsubscribe or mark you as spam).

Pretty cool, right?

Continual Sales Loop™ – Email Offers on Steroids!

This section is perhaps my favourite part of the Mind-Hack™ Marketing method! I LOVE the Continual Sales Loop™ because it flat-out works. After writing hundreds of emails and email sequences over the years, I've learned a thing or two about writing emails that sell.

The classic "sell, sell, sell" approach doesn't work any more – you need to pair pitching with a different angle or different perspective each and every single time. In fact, the amount of money you make is **directly proportional** to the number of times you make an offer to your list or the number of conversion points you have – and this is why the Continual Sales Loop™ is so effective.

Let me start you off with a whole load of ideas so you can get creative – and you'll probably even think of your own. The number one thing to remember is that emails don't need to be boring and they certainly don't need to sound the same.

Add a touch of your own personality in them, but keep them relevant, informative, entertaining or just plain different. Use stories, anecdotes, personal experiences, news stories, current affairs or anything else you can think of.

The key takeaway is that you can literally pitch in every single email as long as every single email is a new and interesting way of sharing the pitch. Your pitches' value and your selling ability will go off the charts!

Email angles are fascinating because you can get super creative with them. For the examples I'm going to share with you below, I'll be focusing on weight loss and how the kind of email you come up with will look different depending on who the persona is.

Here are a few to get you going...

How to X (Benefit) Without Y (Pain Point):

This is a very common angle used by most marketers because it's fool proof. It's a basic benefit-driven angle where you point out the pain they will NOT experience to get the result they want. Here's what this looks like in action:

- **Busy professional:** *How to lose 20lbs in 30 days without spending hours in the gym or kitchen.*
- **New mother:** *How to flatten your baby belly in 30 days without wasting hours in the gym or the kitchen.*
- **Food addict:** *How to lose 20lbs in a month eating delicious food and without starving yourself.*

What to Do if X (Problem):

Another common angle used by marketers. This one speaks directly to the pain point your prospect is facing:

- **Busy professional:** *What to do if you don't have time to go to the gym.*
- **New mother:** *What to do if your baby belly won't shrink.*
- **Food addict:** *What to do if you're addicted to sugar.*

The Myth About X (Problem):

Addressing common myths your prospects have about the problems they're facing works because it's a great opportunity to educate them on something they believe to be true, but isn't. It also gives your prospect a sense of relief – especially if it's something they struggle with. For example:

- **Busy professional:** *The myth about spending hours in the gym.*
- **New mother:** *The myth about shifting baby weight quickly.*
- **Food addict:** *The myth about depriving yourself of your*

favourite foods.

Hopefully you understand how this works: the formula stays the same, but the outcome and the content of your emails will change depending on the persona you have — meaning the ideas you can come up with are almost limitless... it's called Continual Sales Loop™ for a reason!

Now that you can see just how powerful this is, let me go ahead and share some more angles with you:

- **Case Study** — This is particularly good when you have products where there is a high degree of scepticism about your product claims or the product is expensive. Focus on the end result of the case study; for example, if you have a case study of a mother of five kids losing 30lbs in eight weeks, your angle would be, "How a Mother of 5 Kids Lost 30lbs in 8 Weeks." Keep it simple!
- **Testimonial** — Using a testimonial to overcome objections is a great way to help prospects make a buying decision. If you have a testimonial for each objection your prospects have, even better!
- **Your Personal Story** — Nothing is more powerful than your own story, so use it! If you don't have one, you can use a story from one of your customers (with their permission of course).
- **X (Number) Weird Ways to Y (Problem)** — Weird is an interesting angle to use as it plays on curiosity. People are always curious about something that can promise them a particular result. For example: "3 Weird Fruits That Melt Fat From Your Middle!"

- **X (Number) Secret Ways to Y (Problem)** – This makes people feel smart because they think they are privy to something other people don't know about. For example: "5 Secret Exercises to Get Washboard Abs in Record Time."
- **FAQs** – Frequently asked questions are brilliant to use as angles because they give your prospects the information they need to make a decision. For example: "Your Top 10 Questions About Weight Loss Answered."
- **Urgency** – There's nothing quite like urgency to push someone into making a buying decision. Use sparingly, because if you do this all the time, people feel like there is NO real urgency or scarcity and that they can buy your products at any time. Example: "Flash Sale! Take 30% Off All Weight Loss Programmes for the Next 3 Days Only!"
- **Scarcity** – Very similar to urgency, scarcity can get people off the fence and help them make a buying decision. Example: "Get One-to-One Coaching Help to Lose Weight Permanently – Only 10 Spots Left!"

Hopefully, you've now got plenty of ideas on how to sell to your audience repeatedly without wearing them down. You can combine many of these angles together to create your own unique angles, and of course, feel free to try your own!

By the way, I share a total of 29 different angles with you in my Mind-Hack™ Marketing workshop. Go to http://arfasairaiqbal.com/mindhackresources to find out more.

Pre-Selling Your List to Increase Sales

You've probably heard about the idea of pre-selling your

audience, but perhaps you're not sure how to do it.

Pre-selling is the ability to promote a product or a service and have someone emotionally invested in it so they're pre-sold on the idea of buying it. When presented with the opportunity to purchase, they're ready and waiting to make the payment!

There are many versions of pre-selling, and the process can happen offline or online through a variety of different mediums.

Apple have nailed the art of pre-selling – whenever they release the latest version of their iPhone, there are people queuing in the early hours of the morning just so they can be the first to buy.

The same applies to products online. If you've ever wondered why some sales pages convert much better than others, then chances are that the visitors were pre-sold on the information before they hit the sales page.

In a nutshell, pre-selling is about the things that happen BEFORE the sales pitch. It's NOT about pitching. It's about connecting with your customers and helping them to alleviate some sort of problem.

When done correctly, pre-selling means:

- Gaining trust.
- Giving value.

- Creating the right emotional connection.
- Hitting your prospects' hot buttons (the things that bother them the most).
- Helping them understand their problems.
- Eliminating any false beliefs they may have.
- Presenting them with the right information.
- Seeding content to create a natural curiosity for your products.

It's been proven beyond a shadow of a doubt that a pre-sold prospect is far more likely to convert than a cold prospect. That's because pre-selling warms the prospect up by presenting them with tips and solutions that can help solve their biggest problems.

Pre-selling can happen in many ways: through content, webinars, videos etc. However, I want to focus on using pre-selling in your email sequences in particular. You can still apply these principles to any content you produce, but my focus in this section is to really help you write more persuasive emails that pre-sell your prospects BEFORE you send them to your sales page.

This is extremely powerful when done right, because it will make a HUGE difference in the conversion rates of your sales page. It will help to keep your audience engaged and will lower spam complaints and opt-outs.

There are lots of ways of pre-selling – and it all starts with the first touchpoint your intended audience has with you: your lead magnet.

Your lead magnet is also known as an "ethical bribe", an "irresistible offer", an "opt-in bribe" etc. and is basically valuable content you're giving away for free (in exchange for an email address) that solves a problem or enlightens your prospect over a particular issue they may be having.

A lead magnet should form the front-end of a sales funnel. Remember, a sales funnel is simply a process of moving a potential prospect into an actual prospect and then into a buyer and then a repeat buyer.

For example, if you have a product that's aimed at helping new parents get a good night's sleep, your pre-selling strategy might include giving away a free report or video series sharing tips on how to settle new-born babies, so they sleep longer at night.

If your prospects like your content and find it valuable and helpful, they're more likely to buy your product. You can then follow up with a series of email autoresponders (an email sequence) that offer even more value by sharing helpful and relevant advice to parents. The idea is to show prospects what solutions they need... but you're only sharing a tiny bit of the HOW – they have to buy your product to find out the full details!

The idea of your autoresponders is to move a prospect further down your sales funnel and towards your product/ service. You can help do this by revealing some techniques or uses of your product that would solve your prospect's problem.

The way you write your emails is incredibly important. From the language you use, to the various different persuasion techniques you use in them (that's a topic for another day!), your emails are designed to do one thing and one thing only:

Pre-sell your prospects into wanting to buy your product or service BEFORE they hit your sales page.

If you're creating your first-ever series of emails, I recommend writing at least seven emails in your sequence. Never underestimate what it takes to move a prospect into a buyer. You need several touchpoints with your prospect before they decide whether your product/service is right for them.

The aim of your emails is to educate, inform, wow and help prospects make the right decision – seven emails is what I personally recommend and create when I am working with clients. However, I've had clients for whom five or six emails have been enough. I've also had clients who've needed more than 10!

The general advice is that the more expensive the product, the more pre-selling is needed. However, it also depends upon many other factors such as the quality of your list, the kind of lead magnet prospects opted in for, the type of product you're selling etc.

All of these things impact your email sequences. My most recent client is currently in the middle of a product launch and I wrote a total of 26 emails for a $2,000 product!

If you're writing the emails yourself, here are some suggestions on how to pre-sell:

1. **Talk about themes relevant to your product** – Your main aim is to give away a tip or secret and explain the "what" with only a small bit of the "how". You want prospects to think, "Wow, that's great, I need to know this" – and leave out just enough so that they would need to buy your product to find out more.

2. **Give each email a teaser at the end** – Perhaps leave something out and promise to share it with them tomorrow. The way I like to think about it is you want to leave them with a cliff-hanger, just like in your favourite soap: you have to tune in the next day to find out what happens!

3. **NEVER pitch in each email to your prospects** – This is a hard NO. Instead, give them valuable insights into the problems they're facing. In the third or fourth email, you can do a VERY soft pitch. Nothing makes a prospect hit the delete button faster than being bombarded with pitches again and again!

4. **Keep your audience engaged** – Use the P.S. at the end to give your prospects a sneak peek into what they can expect in the next email; this way, they'll want to come back and learn more.

5. **Use attention-grabbing subject lines** – For each email you send out, make the subject line sharp and to the point.

Prospects should think, "I've got to open this and read it." Great headlines should give a big benefit to the prospect, arouse curiosity and should be written in a compelling way. If not, your prospects won't even open your message, let alone read it.

6. **Avoid a hard sell in any sense of the word** – If you've written your email sequence correctly, each one you send out should be edging the prospect naturally towards your product, and you should leave out the full pitch until the final email you send out.

7. **Eliminate alternatives** – Before your final pitch, include an email that eliminates the alternatives. For example, if you have a video product teaching people how to train their dog, your alternatives might include a book (which is too long and doesn't show you visually what to do), hiring a dog trainer (expensive) or going to a training class (expensive, you have to travel to get there, inconvenient, and so on). Once you've eliminated the alternatives, present your product as THE solution for the prospect.

8. **Your full pitch is your last email and should give an overview of your product** – Mention the biggest benefits of your product to your prospect and then point them to your sales page.

For a sequence of seven emails, here's how I would write the emails:

- **Email 1** – Welcome email. Set expectations for your

prospect on how you can help them, what you'll be sending them and how often.

- **Email 2** – Talk about a problem your prospect is having and offer a tip.
- **Email 3** – Mention a false belief your prospect might have about their problem and offer advice.
- **Email 4** – Offer another helpful tip and make a very soft pitch by briefly mentioning your product.
- **Email 5** – Give more valuable content designed to help them understand their problem better and give another tip or recommendation.
- **Email 6** – This email should eliminate any alternatives to your product by talking about their advantages and disadvantages.
- **Email 7** – Full pitch for your product and call to action to check out the sales page.

If you've written your emails correctly, you'll find you get more click-throughs from your email sequence (and then to your "Buy Now" button) than if you were to send visitors to your sales page alone.

The aim of these emails is simple: create enough value and desire that your prospects naturally gravitate towards the actual product itself. The only "hard" sell is in the last email.

Your pre-selling material should push your prospects about 70% of the way towards your product. It's the job of your sales letter to push your prospects over the edge (by overcoming objections, shifting their belief patterns, showing them what's possible etc.) and ensure your product is positioned as the only answer your prospects are looking for.

Pre-selling material plus a well-constructed sales page together form an incredibly powerful combination that can considerably improve your conversion rates and help you sell more of your products and services.

One question I'm often asked is, "Do I need to be a copywriter to write emails?" and the answer is, "Well, that varies!" I truly believe that as long as you're a decent writer, you can definitely learn how to write effective emails that engage your audience and convince them to buy your product.

Keeping Email Engagement High

How do you sell more of your programmes and services without actually annoying and frustrating the people on your list?

That's a tricky question, since most marketers will tell you that the more you place your stuff in front of the right audience, the more people will buy. In fact, when your list becomes tired and non-responsive, the natural solution seems to be to find new people to sell to.

However, growing your list further has an associated cost to it too, which is why you need to get smart about keeping email engagement high.

So here are three things you can immediately do that will help to sell more of your products without the need to spend more on acquiring new customers:

1. *Focus on the Primary Emotions of Your Audience*
What underlying emotional need does your product solve? By figuring out the underlying emotional needs of your audience and connecting these to the benefits of your product, you'll automatically increase the desire for your actual product and you'll be able to sell more of it!

For example, if you sell a weight loss programme, then the emotional need for your clients is that they want to feel confident in their own skin. It's NOT just about losing weight. It's about how they FEEL. By focusing on this in your marketing, you'll sell more of your programmes all day long than by simply saying, "This programme will help you lose weight."

2. *Paint a Picture of What Success and Failure Look Like*
A super-powerful technique to help your audience move from prospects to actual customers is painting a mental picture of what success and failure look like if they DON'T buy your product.

So for our weight loss example, if they buy your programme, they'll be healthier, more energetic and they'll feel confident enough to try new things. If they DON'T use your programme, they'll continue to feel stuck where they are and their health will suffer, meaning they'll miss out on many opportunities in life.

See how powerful this is?

3. *Switch Up Headlines and Subject Lines*

One of the easiest ways to see the biggest gains with your marketing is by switching up your headlines and subject lines in your emails. Make them benefit-oriented and emotional if possible. You want to connect with your prospects' pain points so that when they read your subject lines or headlines they are immediately drawn to your emails. One of my favourite formulas is:

"How to X (Benefit) Without Y (Pain Point/Struggle)"

It's a simple but powerful formula that immediately tells your audience what's in it for them and that they can have it without the pain point they want to avoid the most.

Lastly, don't feel constrained by any one angle – remember, we've already shown in this chapter that there are at least 29 different angles. So get creative and map out all of the angles for each of your personas and then start implementing them. You'll be surprised at how effective they are!

Aside from implementing the Continual Sales Loop™ and using the various angles in your business, there are three more things you can immediately do to prevent list fatigue and disengagement setting in:

1. *Focus on giving value MORE than selling* – This is all about building a relationship, and the law of reciprocity means you MUST give value to your audience first and foremost, before

asking for the sale. This way, emails don't feel salesy and you'll develop better engagement with your emails.

2. *Find different ways to tell your audience about your products without actually "selling"* – For example, if you sell weight loss products, part of your email campaign might include case studies or an interview with people who've successfully lost weight using your products. This not only continues the relationship, but stops you feeling like a second-hand car salesperson!

3. *Segment your list properly* – Some of your list will NOT want your product right now – period. Maybe they don't need it just yet or are very early on in the buying cycle and need more convincing. By only sending sales emails out to people who are opening 80% of your value-added emails, you'll drive the number of sales UP while driving the number of spam complaints DOWN.

By implementing the Continual Sales Loop™ with the tips outlined in this chapter, you'll see a huge improvement in the open and click-through rates of your emails and have better engagement throughout your campaigns.

Summary

In this chapter, I talked about how hammering your list repeatedly with the same kinds of emails asking people to buy is hurting your business.

If you want to get your emails read and responded to, you

need to change tactics and focus on pre-selling and sharing information in different ways, which is also known as the Continual Sales Loop™.

The key takeaways are:

- The amount of money you make is **directly proportional** to the number of times you make an offer to your list or the number of conversion points you have.
- Changing the angle will help you sell your products in multiple ways.
- Making your angles persona specific will increase the number of ways you're able to sell the same product.
- Pre-selling will "sell" your prospects into wanting to buy your product or service without actually directly selling to them.
- Pre-selling is about gaining trust, building a relationship and presenting your prospects with the right information in the right way. This will bring your prospects to the natural conclusion that your product or service is right for them.
- Each of your messages should offer an insight or tip (the WHAT) with only a small bit of the HOW.
- Your email sequences are all about value and the focal point should NEVER be pitching. Instead, concentrate on a very soft pitch around the third or fourth email and a full pitch in your last email.
- It's the job of your sales page to do the actual selling. Pre-selling will push your prospects 70% of the way towards a sale, while your sales page should do the rest.
- With the Continual Sales Loop™, you can create multiple

angles for your different personas and avatars, meaning it's almost impossible to run out of ideas for content!

In the next chapter, we'll be covering irresistible offers – how to ensure you're using the right words to outsell your competition!

Chapter 12: Creating an Irresistible Offer

Selling is always based on emotion – never forget that *people buy on emotion and justify with logic*.

As you saw in an earlier chapter, Steve Jobs had one job – to sell his computer named LISA. Despite taking out a nine-page ad in a national paper, he failed to sell LISA because all he pushed was logic rather than emotion.

This brings me to your offers. How you present your offers will make a HUGE difference in your ability to sell. That's why in this chapter, we're going to delve into the world of copywriting.

Copywriting is simply salespersonship in print or digital media. It's a very specialised skill set – one I've spent over a decade honing and perfecting. In fact, copywriting is a real art, and is even considered to be one of the highest paid skills in the world.

And with good reason. Thanks to copywriters, businesses are able to make a ton of money. We're what you call the "secret sauce" behind multi-million-pound launches.

The words you write to sell (referred to as copy) make a HUGE impact on the number of sales you make. As I've mentioned in previous chapters, I'm a huge fan of direct response marketing which is designed to elicit an immediate response from the audience.

It's All About the Pitch

My earliest memory of watching sales pitches dates back to my childhood when I was about 10 years old. I used to help my father on a market stall selling ladies' fashion items, and there used to be a guy on the stall next to us who would sell car wax and do the most elaborate sales pitches ever. Let's call him Mr Cool.

With a car panel on his table, Mr Cool would roll through his pitch talking about how amazing the car wax was, how it would buff and shine away dullness and minor scratches and how it would protect your car from the elements.

Then Mr Cool did something REALLY cool (hence the name): he would pour lighter fluid on the car panel and tell the audience to stand back – and then he'd proceed to set the panel on fire! It was pretty impressive, even though the fire lasted no more than 10 seconds at best.

After smothering the fire with a cloth, Mr Cool would say, "Voila, the car is as good as new!" before going in for the kill and ushering people to buy. The post-pitch frenzy was like watching sharks on a feeding ground – utterly crazy!

After the last person would buy from him, Mr Cool would take a small break with a cup of tea before doing the whole show again. Each time Mr Cool pitched, I watched in amazement, peeking through the crowd and never getting tired of his pitch.

It was like poetry in motion. Every single line was carefully rehearsed. He knew his lines like the back of his hand. Mr Cool had me mesmerised.

After Mr Cool came the famous late-night TV infomercials. Tony Robbins was one of the first-ever people I watched on these infomercials selling his Personal Power programme – and as a teenager, I was FASCINATED. I didn't know what personal development was back then, but I wanted his programme – I felt like he was promising me the whole world and everything in it. And I wanted a piece of the pie. I BELIEVED him when he said you can have everything you've ever wanted.

In my lifetime, I've probably watched thousands of sales pitches – including many infomercials that I watched multiple times. I would sit there in wonder at how awesome the product must be; and imagine how my life would change if I bought it.

That's the power of a great pitch. It has the power to get you excited and inspire hope. It can move you to take action and buy something on a whim when it wasn't even on your radar before then.

I've seen great marketing campaigns let down by mediocre or weak pitches. The pitch is the highlight or pinnacle of your campaign. It's where everything magically falls together so the prospect can't help but take action.

I remember a couple of years back, I wrote a marketing campaign for one of my long-standing clients. It was done using a series of four videos where the last video was a sales video. We also had a series of emails going out to my client's list about the videos.

One lady emailed my client saying she was "bracing herself" for the sales pitch because she knew it was going to be amazing. This lady ended up buying my client's product. Afterwards, she told my client that she couldn't wait to join his programme because she was "blown away" by how incredible the video series was.

That's the kind of reaction you want potential customers to have when they encounter your sales pitch. A great sales pitch is about tapping into the psychology of your avatars and eliciting an emotional response from your audience.

If you've done that correctly, the likelihood of your audience buying from you is going to be very high – even if it's an "expensive" product.

As a general rule of thumb, the more expensive the product is, the longer the sales pitch needs to be. This is also true in highly competitive industries/highly saturated markets.

The longest sales pitch I've ever written was 30 pages long – and that was to sell a weight loss product. It wasn't the most expensive product I've ever sold; however, this was a product in a VERY saturated market, hence we needed a longer pitch to cover the main elements a person needs to know in order to make an informed buying decision.

How to Win Business Regardless of the Medium You Use

I've talked about this earlier but feel it's worth mentioning again. You must carefully consider the medium you use to deliver your pitch. If you use the wrong medium, your message will never get consumed.

If you use a text-heavy sales page to pitch to an audience that prefers video, they'll never read your sales page. Therefore, it's essential that you figure out if your audience likes to read before using the written word as the preferred sales pitch format.

A huge tip is to have multiple formats for your sales message – that way you're covered regardless. Multiple formats can increase your sales conversion rate because you're increasing the likelihood of someone consuming your message, and therefore buying from you.

So right now you're probably asking what makes a successful sales pitch?

Since 2010, I've written sales pitches with conversion rates as high as 19% from COLD TRAFFIC. **That's an INSANE conversion rate, since the average is around 2–3% online!**

There are lots of frameworks online for writing great sales pitches that convert – but underneath ALL of those frameworks, the basic elements remain the same:

- Explain the problem or desire (the unmet need).
- Agitate or explore the problem/desire.
- Introduce the solution.
- Explain how the solution works.
- Prove your solution works.
- Ask for the sale.

This framework is based on the age-old PAS formula, where PAS stands for "Problem, Agitate, Solution". I've already talked about PAS in Chapter 10 along with a couple of other frameworks for writing the best copy – but this one is my hands-down favourite.

How to Pitch Effectively

There are various ways to pitch – whether it's done in person, on stage, online or over the phone, pitching is a necessary part of the marketing and sales process. If you've done your marketing right, your prospects should be warmed up and ready to be sold to.

Before you even get into the actual sales pitch, you MUST ensure you cover all the things a prospect needs to know about your offer BEFORE you ask for the sale. My Mirror Matrix™ will help you do just that.

The Mirror Matrix™

Whether you're aware of it or not, there are a handful of bare-minimum questions your audience needs to know in order to make an informed buying decision.

Your ads or your content will usually be the first touchpoint a potential customer has with your business – which is why you need to capitalise on these touchpoints as quickly as possible by giving prospects the information they need in order to make a buying decision as quickly as possible.

The easiest way to do that is by using what I call the Mirror Matrix™ – a series of questions you answer for both your prospects and your business. The interesting thing about these questions is that they are at the subconscious level: whether your prospects are aware of them or not, these are the questions they need to know the answers to in order to satisfy the know, like and trust factor.

Here they are:

- **Who** – Who are YOU to solve the problems of your audience?
- **What** – What is your product/solution and what will it do for your prospect?
- **When** – When will your product give them results?
- **Big Picture** – Where else in your prospect's life is being affected by the problem and how does your product overcome this?
- **Resolution** – Why can't your prospect solve their problem? Why is YOUR solution the perfect solution?
- **How** – How is your solution different to other solutions your audience has already tried (and failed at)?
- **The Future** – What's going to happen if your prospect can't solve their problem? What does their life look like when they use your solution?

If you don't answer all of these questions in your marketing process, you're missing a trick and could easily lose out to your competitors.

Your audience is smart – so give them the information they need in order to make an informed buying decision. Not only does this warm prospects up, but it makes the sale so much easier and can easily double or even triple your sales.

You can easily use the PAS formula WITH the Mirror Matrix™ to write your sales page, webinar, video or other copy where you're pitching. In email, you can use this information in the pre-selling sequence BEFORE you pitch to your prospects.

Building Desire for Your Product/Offer

The key to a successful sales pitch is to build desire for the product. Again, there are lots of ways you can do this, but here are five ways to get you started:

1. **FOMO** – One of the easiest ways to create desire for your product is using FOMO or the fear of missing out! Limited editions, flash sales, one-time offers, introductory offers, early-bird deals and even using "out of stock" or "sold out" (put people on a waiting list) can boost demand for your product!

2. **Curiosity** – This works especially well with information and new releases. Indeed, the entire film industry is based on sneak peeks to create curiosity and intrigue. People are nosey by nature and NEED to know what's happening!

3. **Influencers** – Nothing screams "buy me now" more than your favourite celeb or influencer telling you how good a product/service is. The good thing is you no longer have to spend millions to get someone famous to promote you. One influencer is sometimes all you need to promote your offer.

4. **Repetition** – Often overlooked, but repeatedly showing customers your products again and again (in the right context!) can intensify desire. This is exactly why late-night shopping channels do long presentations that last up to an hour where they'll pitch the product several times.

5. **Storytelling** – Stories are unbelievably powerful and can emotionally connect with your audience on a deeper level. Getting your customers to tell their stories of how your product/service has changed their life is one of the most awesome ways to build desire. More about this below!

The Art of a Good Story

I've touched on storytelling several times throughout this book – and with good reason. Stories work incredibly well; and actually, if you're "allergic" to the idea of selling, then using stories is perfect for you.

Regardless of whether or not you enjoy selling, stories can make your sales pitch that much more powerful. Your prospects naturally have their sales guards UP when someone pitches to them.

Stories, however, bypass the part of your brain that tells you that you're being sold to – and this means you automatically lower your sales guard. Think about it: if you were listening to a great story, you'd enjoy the story and you certainly wouldn't feel like you were being sold to. The same is true for your prospects.

But how do you sell with a story? Here's a simple nine-step framework you can use to share your story as follows:

1. What happened? Share your struggle.
2. When did it happen?
3. Where did it happen?
4. Why did it happen?
5. Emotions – how did it make you feel?
6. Breaking Point – what was the point in your story where you realised there was no turning back or that things had to change?
7. Change – what did you do differently?
8. Epiphany – what was your "aha" moment?
9. Resolution – what was the outcome and how did it make you feel? Be specific about your results!

Stories can easily be used for every element of your marketing, and they work especially well with videos and webinars. Talking of webinars, I have a very specific way of structuring webinars so they sell like crazy – and it involves using storytelling.

Selling via Webinars

There's an art to getting a webinar right. Of all the different kinds of marketing campaigns you can run, webinars tend to have the highest return – and are especially effective if you sell high-ticket products or services.

However, there are three problems. Firstly, they are notoriously difficult to get right. A great webinar needs to be structured properly in order to maximise your chances of success.

Secondly, depending on your industry, webinar fatigue is a thing. Try calling your webinar a masterclass, workshop, training or web class – whatever works for your industry.

Lastly, getting registrations (especially off Facebook) is notoriously expensive. You typically need to have a large budget to get a decent number of registrations for your webinar.

Now, lots of experts will tell you they have the perfect formula for a webinar that converts – and all of them are right in their own way.

The following elements are COMMON among ALL the webinar teachers out there:

- Hook
- Problem
- Story

- Teaching/training
- Your solution
- Pitch
- Testimonials
- Call to action.

Each marketer has their own name/terminology for each of these elements – but the underlying structure is always the same. The cool thing about this framework, however, is that you can actually use it to sell from the stage too – it's just as powerful!

Over the years, I've crafted countless webinars that sell like crazy, so here are my seven steps to creating an awesome webinar (which incorporates storytelling):

1. Your opening sequence and hook – Craft a compelling title that offers a huge benefit or transformation for the audience. Your hook is your big promise – what are you looking to solve for your prospect? The more intriguing your promise, the better the hook!

2. Reveal your struggle – People don't like those who appear to be perfect, which is why it pays to share your personal struggles and failures with your audience. Share your story of how you found the answer to the problem your prospects are having.

3. Highlight the problem – What's the big problem prospects are facing? What are they REALLY struggling with?

4. Introduce the solution – What's the solution to the problem? How can your content speak to the problem your audience is experiencing? What insights, secrets, strategies, etc. can you share with the audience to demonstrate your power? Can you share proof (e.g. reviews) that these work?

5. Reveal the offer – This is where you transition into your pitch! Stack on the value with lots of bonuses to really make your offer stand out. Add in scarcity or urgency to encourage people to buy from you.

6. Eliminate risk – Use a money-back guarantee or continuation of service if the outcome for the client isn't met.

7. Ask for the sale and make it irresistible! – Asking for the sale is an art! Be confident and really share the huge benefits and transformation that your offer provides. Ask for the sale with a CLEAR call to action and TELL people what you want them to do next (e.g. "Click the button below to get started").

You can add in "trial closes" (more about these below) where you present different scenarios designed to get people to agree with you on why your solution is THE solution for them, and then ask for the sale.

In a face-to-face selling situation, trial closes can take the form of questions that are designed to gauge the "temperature" of where someone is when buying...

Because the last thing you want to do is pitch to someone when they aren't ready to buy!

Just to be 100% clear, a trial close is NOT the same as asking for the sale! A trial close is used to simply shift the way someone feels about your offer and to make them more inclined to buy from you.

Here are some of the most common trial closes:

1. If All X (Your Offer) Did Was Y (Benefit) Then Would It Be Worth It to You?

I LOVE this trial close because you pose a series of questions that focus on the BIG BENEFITS of what you're offering. The trick to getting this to work is to ask questions that are relevant to the DESIRED outcome your prospect wants.

So if you had a weight loss programme, this could look like this:

If all Herbalicious did was eradicate your sugar cravings, would it be worth it to you?

If all Herbalicious did was shift stubborn belly fat effortlessly, would it be worth it to you?

If all Herbalicious did was help you shed 20lbs in 10 days, would it be worth it to you?

2. Does This Make Sense to You/Do You See How Powerful This Is?

Here, you're getting people to agree with you because

agreement predisposes people to buy from you. This is especially effective when selling via webinars or on a stage – you're looking for agreement from your audience.

3. Imagine if You Had This Offer X Years Ago, What Would Your Life Look Like Today?

This trial close forces people to think about how their life would have been different had they used your product X years ago. It's a subtle but powerful psychological shift in getting someone to think about their future, without actually telling them to!

Now, while these trial closes are powerful in their own right, there are lots of ways you can use even MORE trial closes in your webinar/pitch/presentation:

- Ask your audience questions throughout your presentation where they agree with what you are saying.
- Ask for participation ("give me a yes if you agree with me").
- Tell people to raise their hands in response to a LOADED question (such as "raise your hand if you can see Herbalicious working for you").

Remember, with a trial close, you're NOT asking for the sale – you're helping to predispose prospects to buy from you by shifting their behaviour on a subconscious level.

Three Ways of Asking for the Sale After a Consultation or Strategy Session

Now, if you're an expert who sells high-ticket programmes and you're not confident about pitching, my advice to you would be to avoid pitching on the webinar and push for getting people to book a strategy call or consultation with you instead.

It's SO much easier than trying to craft a killer sales pitch – which can be difficult to pull off if you don't know what you're doing. Instead, make the call seem like it's packed with advice that's going to benefit the prospect.

If you sell the call well, it should be relatively easy to get as many people booking calls with you as possible. You can then pitch to your prospects after the call.

I don't like using the term "discovery call" – which is a fancy way of saying "sales call" – your prospects aren't stupid and will immediately feel as if you're trying to pitch to them. Discovery calls are much harder to "sell" than a consultation/ strategy call – even if you're giving these away for free!

That's because with a consultation/strategy call, the very name implies you're going to help your prospect. And that's exactly what these calls should be. You can also try the term "clarity call" because clarity is very powerful.

When a prospect is stuck and doesn't know why, giving them clarity on WHY they are stuck is just as powerful as giving someone the answers. Once you've delivered your strategy session, you can then transition into your pitch and close prospects on the call.

I don't know about you, but my first attempts at closing on a call were HORRIBLE – I had NO idea what I was doing and would come across as being "pushy" (as one guy told me!).

NOT COOL!

Thankfully, that was a VERY long time ago – and since then, I've honed the ability to sell even very high multi-five-figure deals over the phone without EVER coming across as pushy or salesy.

So here are some of my favourite ways to ask for the sale:

1. Ask if They Need Help

I LOVE this because it's an effortless way to move people into asking for the sale – but without feeling pushy. The easiest way to transition into asking for the sale is to FIRST use a trial close such as:

"Did you find this helpful?"

If they say yes, then simply say, *"Ok great! Is this something you'd like my help with?"*

90% of the time, they will say yes – and that's your cue to tell them about your programme and how it works.

So easy!!!

2. Give Your Prospects Choice

I once had a sales call with an incredible copywriter who closed me and I didn't even know what had happened! I was so stunned with how beautifully he asked for the sale that, years later, I've never forgotten what he did!

He asked me a simple question:

"If you were likely to go ahead, would you prefer a payment plan or paying in full?"

To which I responded "payment plan"... and this is when the magic happened...

"Ok great! Will that be Visa or Mastercard?"

I nearly fell off my chair! The close was so effortless and easy that I didn't know what hit me!

This is such an EASY way to close a potential client because it's based on giving the client full choice and control.

3. The Silent Close

The silent close is one of my favourite closes – because it's based on you staying SILENT while the prospect thinks about it!

At the end of your pitch, you simply ask two questions. The first question is, "How does that sound?" You're listening for the prospect to say something positive before moving on to the second question which is this:

"Would you like to go ahead?"

... and then say NOTHING!

Not a SINGLE word.

The silence creates tension which might feel awkward for you – however, it gives your prospect much-needed space to think. It's non-threatening and shows you have respect for their decision.

You might be tempted to talk in the space, but don't! This one takes a little bit of practice because the first few times you do this, it's going to feel weird – but I promise you it isn't!

Overcoming Objections

Ok, you've done the hard work and delivered your pitch. Now the likely scenario is you'll probably encounter some kind of objection before you can close successfully.

When potential customers say they can't afford you, what they REALLY mean is they're not sure if they can go ahead. Something is stopping them from saying yes – and it's usually something emotional.

At this point, you're probably sick of hearing me say this, but the reason is because people buy on emotion and justify with logic...

Therefore, you must address the underlying issues that could be preventing someone from buying your products and experiencing a transformation.

Objections over money are rarely the REAL issue – so don't be tempted to discount!

Here are four things you SHOULD be doing instead, which you can use in both your pitch with a prospect on a call or even on your sales page:

1. Link your offer to an outcome the customer wants and try to connect it to something emotional.

E.g. "You'll learn how to control your sugar cravings so you can drop unwanted pounds quickly and feel more confident in your own skin."

"So you can" is a great connecting phrase between what your product will do for them and the benefits and outcomes the customer wants.

Notice how I mentioned the big benefit ("drop unwanted pounds") and attached the emotional aspect to it as well ("feel more confident").

Repeat this for all the outcomes and desires your customer

wants.

2. Offset the objection by comparing the price to something familiar and linking it to the customer's end goal.

E.g. "For the price of a takeaway, you're getting everything you need to totally transform your body and get in the best shape of your life."

By comparing the price to something familiar, you're allowing people to come to the natural conclusion that, actually, the price is no big deal. Now the caveat here is for very large investments – when you get to anything past the 10k mark, this one becomes difficult to pull off.

3. For larger purchases, acknowledge the price as an investment into their future outcome.

E.g. "I understand that £3,000 is a lot of money, but it's an investment into your health and wellbeing."

Link this investment to a fear/frustration or dream/desire the prospect has and pose this as a question.

E.g. "Let me ask you, are you really going to let your sugar cravings control your life and leave you with the possibility of developing diabetes or heart disease in later life?"

This tip works really well for sales pages and pitches online/ on stage – but might feel awkward over a call (in which case you should use the next tip instead).

4. Pre-suppose they can afford the investment by first acknowledging it's a lot of money and then asking if they would invest if they had it.

E.g. "I understand that £3,000 is a lot of money, but it's an investment into your health and wellbeing. If you could easily afford the programme without money being an object, would you go ahead?"

It's VERY rare for a qualified prospect to say no to this question! When they say yes, immediately ask them, "Why?"

Then stay quiet while the prospect tells you why they want your offer. You want to repeat back to them the reasons they've given you and THEN try to figure out how to make the money a non-issue with a payment plan or deposit etc.

You'll notice in all of these examples, the central theme is EMOTION.

By learning how to tap into the emotions your prospect is feeling, you'll effortlessly turn more leads into buyers.

Common Mistakes When Pitching

Selling your products using benefits (especially emotional benefits) is critical since your prospects need to know what's in it for them – and without these benefits, you'd have a hard time selling anything...

However, it's just as important for you to tap into the

deepest, darkest fears your prospects have and bring those to the surface...

The reason for this is simple: it balances out your sales copy/ pitch and gives prospects a reason to act now – but only when you do it right!

If you get it wrong, using fear in your copy can sadly have the **opposite effect** of what you're trying to achieve.

Specifically, there are **five common mistakes** businesses make when using fear in their copy or their pitch:

1. Focusing on the Wrong Fear

Everyone has some kind of fear that keeps them up and takes over their thoughts in the dead of the night. Focus on what this is – not something that might not even be on their radar or plane of awareness.

Creating a new situation you "think" they fear is a sure way to get your sales message ignored.

2. Using Future Fears That Don't Resonate

We all know that too much chocolate and too many sweets will eventually rot our teeth and give us diabetes, but this doesn't stop sweet manufacturers from making billions from their products.

Knowing the risk rarely motivates us to change our behaviour because the threat is not imminent. That's because the instant pleasure outweighs any future fear that COULD happen years or even decades from now.

Therefore, focus on the fear that's more likely to happen immediately, rather than in some distant future.

3. Using Too Much Fear

Fear in your copy should be handled like seasoning: you need to use the right amount. Too much is too much and can put people off buying from you.

Too much fear comes across as doom and gloom and can literally "freeze" your prospect into taking no action at all. Instead, maintain a more balanced approach and also focus on what prospects have to gain.

4. Using Fears That Can't Be Solved Quickly

There's always SOMETHING to be afraid of – but focusing on fears that can't be solved as quickly as possible won't give your prospects any reason to buy.

There's no point in pushing your audience's panic buttons unless you can show how your product eliminates the cause of this fear as quickly and as painlessly as possible.

5. All Fear, No Payoff

Copy that only focuses on fear without giving a payoff will

have a hard time selling anything. Your campaigns shouldn't really be about the fear unless you're in a market that demands this, such as security or pharmaceuticals.

Rather, your message should talk about the solution to that fear.

Most people won't buy just because they're afraid... they buy because your product can really help them and stop them from experiencing any fear in the process.

In short, when it's done properly, fear WITH payoff can really motivate prospects to buy now.

Another common mistake when pitching is to talk over your prospects. This is especially important when you're taking a sales call. Talking over your prospects, or indeed talking too much, is a sign that you lack confidence when pitching.

One of the worst mistakes you can make when pitching to someone who says they don't have the money is to use phrases like, "If your family member was sick and needed an urgent operation and you had to get the money somehow, wouldn't you?"

This one sounds weird, but believe me it's been used on me several times! It's probably one of the most uncomfortable ways to pitch to someone. Not only does it come across as pushy and salesy, but I would go as far as to say this is what you would class as a "hard" sell.

In other words, an awful experience! Now, there may be some gurus who tell you that this is the right way to do sales – and I would challenge that heavily. I've personally sold clients multi-five-figure projects without such aggressive sales tactics.

Summary

In this chapter, we covered ways to make your offer irresistible. Specifically, I talked about the following:

- There are multiple ways you can present your offer, including sales pages, webinars and even speaking from the stage.
- Remember the golden rule – people love to buy, but hate being sold to.
- Make the sales pitch as easy and effortless for prospects as possible so they feel empowered to make the right decision for THEM.
- Prospects should NEVER be pushed or guilt-tripped into buying.

In the next and final chapter, we're going to take a look at the most common mistakes businesses make when executing their marketing campaigns.

Chapter 13: Common Mistakes Businesses Make

In this chapter, we'll take a look at some of the most common mistakes businesses make when executing marketing campaigns. We've spent a LOT of time figuring out the ideal client and understanding how to plan your campaigns.

Specifically, we covered sales funnels in detail and how you can give yourself the best chance of success with a profitable funnel.

However, sometimes things don't work as they should – for lots of different reasons. Along your customer journey, a number of issues could be at fault:

- Your offer could be wrong.
- Your copy isn't compelling enough.
- You haven't qualified prospects properly.
- The wrong people are on your list.
- Something is broken.
- The ads aren't working as they should.

There are literally so many things that could potentially be off, not to mention tech issues. This is why optimising, testing and tweaking your campaigns and funnels is a MUST.

In fact:

- Big-name marketers are CONSTANTLY optimising their

funnels before they find the winner.

- Optimisation can take several months (and for some people, can take years).
- Every time you optimise, you need to test your funnel, which can burn through money faster than you can say "leaky bucket"!
- The amount of money you spend on getting your funnel perfect can end up running into the thousands or more.

To put things in perspective, I once worked with a client where it took almost a year and several rounds of split testing to find the right funnel – and we were spending around £3,000 a MONTH testing!

Most big-name marketers will sometimes run more than a hundred tests to find the winning combination of copy and images etc! Remember, the right campaign is where you put £1 in and get at LEAST £2 out!

Technicalities aside, there are many other factors that can also affect conversion rates on campaigns, such as time of year, whether the product is seasonal – even what the weather is like!

Many business owners forget that numbers and data are actually people – and people's behaviour can be impacted by so many things. For example, the sale of strawberries and cream goes through the roof when Wimbledon takes place.

Sales of beer and snacks shoot up during football season. Sales of sunscreen soar during the summer months but drop in the winter. If you are in the weight loss niche, you'll find yourself busiest during the run-up to Christmas, in the New Year and the summer. You get the idea!

So this brings me on to you – you've put a lot of effort into your campaigns, but something isn't working as it should and this means you've got bottlenecks that need fixing.

In the table below, you can see a high-level overview of some of the most common problems when creating campaigns and what the most likely causes and fixes are.

Problem	Potential Causes	Potential Fixes
Lots of traffic, not enough ad clicks.	Wrong audience. Copy angle doesn't work.	Test new audiences. Test multiple copy angles.
Lots of traffic and clicks to ads, but not enough leads.	Landing page copy doesn't work. Offer isn't compelling enough.	Change the copy. Change the design of the landing page.
Not enough traffic.	Low opportunity volume (usually restricted by too narrow targeting).	Broaden your audience targeting and test lookalike audiences.

Problem	Potential Causes	Potential Fixes
Poor open rates on emails.	Poor subject lines. Wrong people on list. Email content doesn't resonate. Emails not being delivered (hitting junk or never arriving).	Test subject lines. Test new audiences. Go back to your avatar and ensure you're writing great content. Check your SPF/ DMARC and DKIM settings.
No one clicking through emails to sales page or call booking page.	Wrong people on list. Email content doesn't resonate. No call to action/ poor call to action. Poor pitch.	Check ideal client. Work on relevant content. Ensure good calls to action and test multiple ones. Give emotional reasons why someone needs to buy/book a call.
High unsubscribe/ spam rates on emails.	Emails badly written or irrelevant.	Focus on relevancy. Hire a copywriter.
High leads, high engagement on emails, high click through rates, but no one is buying.	Sales page/pitch is badly written or irrelevant. Poor pitch. Poor offer. Confusing sales process. People unable to buy (broken links/ process).	Focus on relevancy. Test new copy. Hire a copywriter. Test purchase buttons. Switch up your offer. Simplify the sales process with clear instructions.

There are SO many potential issues a campaign might encounter, the mind boggles – but this is exactly the reason why testing and split testing are critical.

However, there's a right way to split test and a wrong way to do it. The wrong way is testing multiple things at once – and worse, not keeping a log of what you did and what you changed.

I speak from painful experience. One of the first funnels I tried to optimise, I managed to break it because I made far too many changes at the same time. No matter how hard I tried, I couldn't undo the changes I had made. This meant a funnel that was once working just didn't work any more.

For split testing, here are some tips to ensure you do it right:

- Start with testing headlines and subject lines – they're the easiest things to change and test and usually have the biggest impact in terms of results.
- Only test ONE thing at a time – and run enough traffic through it to check if the improvement worked before moving on to the next test.
- Log and date EVERY SINGLE change made, tracking results as you go.
- Calls to action should also be tested – the first thing to test is the call to action itself, then the colour/shape of buttons.
- Images for ads and landing pages are tested next.
- Test offers next if everything else is working but people are still not buying – test different price points and even

discounts, bonuses etc.

- The LAST thing to test should be the copy itself – if in doubt, always get an experienced copywriter to check over your copy first.
- Test the entire funnel from start to finish to ensure nothing is broken and that everything is firing as it should.
- Lastly, be patient! It can take a lot of trial and error to get a funnel optimised and working really well.

If you need help with optimisation and split testing, you can find out more by going to: http://arfasairaiqbal.com/mindhackresources.

Other Common Mistakes That Businesses Make

One of the biggest mistakes I've seen throughout my career in marketing is not getting 100% clear on your ideal customer. Hopefully after going through this book, this shouldn't be a problem for you.

From experience though, I've lost count of the number of businesses I've worked with that claim they know their ideal client but really don't. For example, one of the most common things I've seen clients do is focus on the very surface-level benefits of what they offer when pitching. Either that or they simply don't dig deep enough into what their customers REALLY want.

Ideal customers aside, another common mistake is trying to write the copy yourself when you simply don't have the skills to do it. While I've shared lots of frameworks and tips throughout this book, sadly, not everyone has a good written style.

In fact, one of my previous clients contacted me after almost two whole years of "trying to figure it out" for himself. When I asked him why he didn't get help sooner, he said he was trying to save money! Thinking like this has an opportunity cost attached to it. In this case, the opportunity cost was in lost sales.

A good copywriter is never an expense – a huge mistake business owners make! A good copywriter will MAKE you money, so you get a good return on your investment.

Do copywriters get it right 100% of the time? No – no they don't. Even some of the best copywriters in the world don't hit a home run every single time. It can take months of testing to find the winning copy angle.

Speaking of copy, here's another HUGE mistake many businesses make, and that's hiring content writers to write copy. Let me be 100% clear on this:

Copy and Content Are NOT the Same!

I've seen so many businesses BURNED by bad writers who try to pass off content as copy. In fact, a good friend of mine lost out on over £30,000 when she hired a content writer to write copy for her business.

The result?

Not. One. Single. Sale...

Ouch.

Needless to say, he was fired!

Content is designed to educate and inform, whereas copy is designed to sell and get people to take action. These are two VERY different skill sets!

Years ago, when I first started out, I was hired by an agency where I had ONE job: to correct the copy written by other writers! This was a growing agency that had hired several writers whose copy was so bad, they couldn't possibly use it for their paying clients.

When I had a call with the agency owner, he admitted to hiring cheap content writers to save money – and it ended up costing him in embarrassment, poor conversion rates, no sales, and angry clients instead.

Too many times I've seen business owners try to "save money" by either hiring content writers to write their copy... Or they try to do it themselves when they have no clue what they're doing... and then they wonder why they aren't making money!

Hiring the wrong person, or trying to do it yourself when you have no experience, has an associated cost attached to it – and it can work out WAY more expensive than hiring a pro.

A good copywriter is NOT expensive: they are an investment in your business!

You might pay a pro £5,000, £10,000 or even more... you might even pay out royalties... but when you see the sales start rolling in and your bank account growing by the day, you'll know you did the right thing.

Either that or you level up and learn how to sell properly. Or, if you want to go broke like my friend almost did, you can simply get a cheap content writer to "save" you money.

This leaves you with two choices: you can either hire a copywriter or learn how to write copy yourself. If you're trying to grow your business, the likelihood is you're ALREADY very busy and probably don't have the time to learn.

If you're going to hire a copywriter, then there are several pitfalls you need to look out for. The biggest thing you need to take into consideration is their level of experience. Has the copywriter written different kinds of campaigns? Have they got experience in your industry?

Does the copywriter understand conversion rate optimisation and how to split test properly? Don't just ask for samples of work – you want to see evidence of how their copy has performed. What kind of conversion rates have they been able to get their clients? Are clients happy with their performance? Does the copywriter have lots of testimonials that state actual results and not just "fluffy" testimonials where clients are saying how nice they are!

As you can see, there's a TON to consider when hiring a copywriter. Lastly, cheap copywriters can end up costing you a lot of money. There's a saying that if you pay peanuts, you'll get a monkey. Truth be told, there are loads of copywriters out there, but finding good ones is surprisingly hard.

A good copywriter who gets results will often come at a price (or should I say investment!). Ask for recommendations from trusted advisers and make sure you hire someone who is known for results.

Summary

In this chapter, I covered the most common mistakes businesses make when marketing. Here's a recap of everything:

- All good marketing campaigns need optimisation and split testing to make them even better.
- When split testing and optimising, always test ONE thing at a time and track everything carefully.
- Funnel failure can very often be down to a number of different factors, and your job is to figure out the cause of the problem and plug the leak as quickly as possible.
- Not digging deep with your avatar is a huge and costly mistake.
- Copy and content are NOT the same thing – they require two very different skill sets.
- A good copywriter is always an investment in your business.

Finally, if you follow the principles in this chapter, you should feel more confident about split testing and optimisation and how to deal with failing campaigns.

Final Thoughts

The needs of your ideal customer should be the driving force behind ALL of your marketing campaigns. Everything you do and everything you create should be 100% guided by the needs of your ideal customer.

Knowing the power of your ideal customer is like having the keys to the proverbial kingdom of riches. If you truly understand this and implement everything I've shared with you in this book, you'll be well ahead of your competitors and can look forward to growing your business strategically and, more importantly, profitably – and this is exactly what Mind-Hack™ Marketing is all about.

What I've shared with you is based on what I've learned over more than a decade of being in the trenches with hundreds of different businesses across multiple industries around the world – including well-known brands and influencers.

I hope you've enjoyed reading this book as much as I've enjoyed bringing it to you. My sincere hope is that you feel excited about the possibilities for your business once you've understood your ideal customer in detail.

With love,

Arfa

Epilogue by Adil Amarsi

A final word by Adil Amarsi from GreatestCopywriterAlive. com:

I've worked in marketing and copywriting for as long as I can remember.

In that time I've consumed more books and courses on marketing and advertising than most – thankfully I can remember a lot of it, so when I write the next sentence, realise this is from decades of knowledge...

Mind-Hack™ Marketing is one of the best books you'll find that will help you apply the concepts of marketing and advertising in your business.

More importantly, this isn't JUST A BOOK, this is a guide.

Meaning it's timeless.

What Arfa Iqbal has shared with you here can be applied today and 50 years into the future!

The resources, ideas, strategies and ALMOST PAINT-BY-NUMBERS approach will allow anyone who applies the advice inside this book to unlock a hidden level of wealth in their business.

Or if you're just starting out, this book will give you the foundation, the roadmap and the tools you need – not to mention instructions on how to use the tools – to build a successful business.

Having generated over a combined $1.2 billion in sales for my clients, customers and followers, I have seen more than most when it comes to advertising and what works.

This book is one of the best you'll find on the market.

A final word of advice...

There are two things I would advise you to do:

1. Go through this book, step by step, and make this a six-month commitment – where you'll be in six months after applying this book will astound you and those around you.
2. For every one hour of reading and study, ensure you put in two hours of effort. Meaning for every bit of studying, double your application time.

Combining these two pieces of advice, you will find yourself having more consistent months, having the grit to keep going when times are tough, and ultimately, having the business you've always wanted.

This is a playbook on how people think, research and respond.

Don't try to reinvent the wheel – apply *Mind-Hack™ Marketing* to your business today and watch what happens.

About the Author

Arfa Saira Iqbal is a multi-nine-figure copywriter, digital marketing consultant and published author who specialises in helping businesses to scale using sales funnels.

Since 2010, Arfa has been helping her clients (including many well-known brands) achieve brilliant results using her skills in direct response copywriting, sales funnels and pre-selling mastery – skills that hinge heavily on being able to understand how customers think.

Arfa has sold products and services across a wide range of industries both online and offline and, together with her "ninja" team, works with clients all over the world to dramatically increase their sales and ROI.

In her spare time, Arfa loves travelling, walking, reading and geeking out on all things marketing. She enjoys spending time with her two boys Jamal and Amaan who would say their mum is as crazy as they are!

Resources & Recommendations

I highly recommend joining my Facebook group "High-Ticket Consulting: Marketing & Sales Insights into 7 Figure Businesses" where I help you get results with your marketing.

Here's what you'll get inside the group:

- Video tear-downs of funnels, websites, copy and more
- Q&A videos
- Tips, advice, resources
- Advice on growing your business
- Live training
- Interviews with entrepreneurs
- Plus so much more!

Join the group here: https://www.facebook.com/groups/mindhackmarketing.

Funnel Services

Want your very own sales funnel but don't know where to start? Check out https://funnelinabox.co.uk/ which gives you all the details of how you can get started with your very own sales funnel in as little as seven working days.

If you want our incredible team to build an entire system for you, please go to http://arfasairaiqbal.com/mindhackresources for more information.

Coaching and Consulting Services

We've got a number of different solutions designed to help you scale with expert positioning and sales funnels with our done-for-you and do-it-yourself programmes. Simply go to http://arfasairaiqbal.com/mindhackresources to learn more.

Printed in Great Britain
by Amazon